For Lou Watson
Enjoy!

1/21/82

AMERICAN C

LASSIC CARS

OF AUTOMOBILES AND MEN

The Duesenberg rolled slowly towards me where I waited on the immense lawn with my camera ready. Moisture from the freshly-cut grass made the tires shiny black. Behind the car, in the distance, rose the white facade of a wealthy man's home. Four hundred idling horsepower produced a deep resonant thunder as the car moved closer, sunrays ricocheting in cascades of light from the chromed radiator. Through the viewfinder, it looked like a hundred flash bulbs had gone off. The glamorous automobile was once owned by a famous moviestar. Today it is perfectly restored—more magnificent looking than ever. A "Survivor"!

The Auburn Speedster stood there on the pier, resting heavily on the weathered planking, deserted by everyone but the seagulls. There was something special about this automobile. Something touching. The black paint job was definitely home-done, the chromed grill had turned reddish brown from the small rust bubbles on it, and the upholstery had been redone in vinyl with a pattern suitable for a kitchen chair but out of character with the Auburn. The old-timer hardly seemed like something to photograph for a book on classic cars. But as I looked closer, I began to understand its special charm. The signs of one man's devotion were evident everywhere; a man who had been faithful to this car for almost fifty years. This made the car very special. A "Survivor"!

Manhattan skyscrapers looked like an army of giants against the yellowing afternoon sky, their almost frightening enormity doubled by the mirror

image in the East River. The cream colored Cord was parked at an angle to the dock but parallel with the Brooklyn Bridge behind it. Dock workers on their way home, fascinated by the beautiful automobile, had stopped and were standing in groups against the warehouse wall behind me, as I searched for the best camera angle. Just when I signalled that I was ready, a man in his seventies emerged from one of the groups by the warehouse. He was dressed in a big trench-coat and walked slowly over to the car. He turned around, folded his arms over his chest and leaned against the Cord, looking straight into the camera. It was a proud pose. I took several frames in rapid sequence. He was the designer of the Cord. Forty years ago he had shaped these forms. He had run his hands a thousand times over the clay model, feeling the smoothness of the curves. He was the creator of one of the milestones in automotive design. A "Survivor"!

Once the Cadillac had been backed out, there was room for both of us to walk into the garage. It was dark inside, but after my eyes had adjusted to the contrast in light, I could see rusty fenders, wheels with-out tires, tires without wheels, boxes overflowing with engine parts, paint cans—all the things which clutter a restorer's garage. The man who showed me around, the owner of the 1929 Cadillac, had a very suntanned face. It carried the definite lines of discipline and determination. He spoke with authority about cam-shafts, carburetors, springblades and runningboards. He told me that he had found the Cadillac a long time ago rusting away in a shack by the Mississippi River. He described how he had taken the car apart, how he had restored every detail with his own hands, and how he had then put it all together again. It had taken years of patient labor. He had sacrificed eve-nings and weekends, but he was the kind of man who had an irresistable urge to preserve the past. A "Survivor"!

With these vignettes I wanted to illustrate, rather than simply describe the spectrum of cars and people represented in this book. Here is the over-restored car, but also the unrestored original. Here is the mass-

produced, but also the one-of-a-kind. Here is the man who has the means to pay others to restore his cars, but also the man who does all the work himself. Here is the designer, the racedriver, the coach builder, the collector—all part of that gigantic mural of cars and people making up the classic car world in America.

A year ago I spent the summer in Europe, criss-crossing England and the Continent in search of "Survivors" for my first book about European Classics. This summer, having the opportunity to do the same in the United States, for a book about American Classics, I was curious as to what I would find. I was not disappointed! The American cars followed a tradition of innovative engineering and displayed trademarks of tasteful design and genuine craftsmanship as fine as the European cars. The owners had the same enthusiasm and dedication as their European counterparts, and they were surprisingly untouched by commercialism. I want to thank all these owners in a special way. They shared their experiences with me. They sometimes let me spend entire days with their cars to photograph them. They let me choose from old pictures in their private photo albums—without their enthusiasm, this book would not have been possible.

I also wish to thank Brian Firth and William Snyder for supplying technical and historical data about the cars and for reviewing parts of the manuscript. Others who, through their contributions, have helped shape the form of the book are John Ansted, Dean Batchelor, Randy Ema, Ulf Erenius, John Fugate, Dave Granados, Bill Kinsman, Strother MacMinn, Everett Miller, Leroy Miller, Cameron Peck, James Rasmussen, Shirley Rusch and Perry Schreffler.

The Duesenberg, introduced in 1921, was a truly race-bred automobile. It was the first race car to average 100 mph for the full distance of the Indianapolis 500. After E. L. Cord took over in 1926 he instructed Fred Duesenberg to develop a car that would be the biggest, fastest, most luxurious and technically advanced on the road. This car, introduced in 1928, was the Model J. Its 420 cubic inch, dual over-head camshaft, straight-eight engine produced 265 hp—more than double that of any other American car. Even the heaviest limousines could top 100 mph, while the lighter sedans and open cars of the supercharged SJ model could hit 100 mph in second gear and 130 in high.

Every Duesenberg body was custom built to reflect the individual taste of the owner. All this elegance and power was not without cost, however. Fitted with custom bodies, the cars commanded prices that ranged between $13,000 and $19,000. In 1936 a Duesenberg with a specially shortened wheelbase was developed, based on the designs of a record-breaking car prepared for Ab Jenkins. Driving a specially streamlined version, he shattered the old one-hour speed records by averaging an impressive 152 mph. Of these cars, designated SSJ, only two were made—one went to Gary Cooper, and the other one went to Clark Gable. Today Gable's car belongs to Al Ferrara of Cleveland, Ohio, and is featured here as a "Survivor".

Named after its Indiana home town, the Auburn was the product of an outgrowth by the Eckhart Carriage Company. This firm, like many others, had decided to convert from hay-burner power to gasoline power. This was, after all, 1900—a new century and a time for new ideas. By building rugged and reliable cars, the company struggled along into the Twenties. In 1924, however, E. L. Cord came on the scene and rapidly turned things around. Sales doubled in 1925 and doubled again the following year.

In the Auburn, Cord gave the public a medium-priced car with a good deal more elegance than some of the higher priced automobiles had. To match the superlative styling, the engineers designed a strong chassis, built to meet all challengers in stock car competition. In March of 1928, for example, the newly introduced Speedster reached an impressive 108 mph at Daytona Beach.

But the Depression affected production of the Auburn—a smaller line of cars was brought out in 1931. The star of the showroom was still the Speedster, such as this 1932 "Survivor" photographed in Santa Barbara, California, and belonging to Helen Keys. Her husband bought it new and it has been his ever since. Auburn engines, built by Lycoming, were straight-eights, and reached a power output of 100 hp at 3400 rpm. Rolling on the last genuine knock-off wire wheels the Speedster combined style and power in a way that made a lasting impression on everyone who saw it.

DUESENBERG 1936

AUBURN 1932

Two American luxury cars, Cadillac and Lincoln, remain in production today. Both of them were founded by the same man, Henry M. Leland. He started with Cadillac, producing the first one in 1902. It quickly attained preeminence. This rise was greatly brought about by its winning the coveted Dewar Trophy both in 1906 (for standardization of parts) and in 1913 (for pioneering work in electrical starting, lighting and ignition). Cadillac introduced their V-8 in 1914 and have kept that configuration to this day. Even during their V-12 and V-16 period, the V-8 was the breadwinner.

In 1926 a young stylist from California, Harley Earle, was brought to General Motors. He was assigned to give Cadillac a new look that matched the flamboyance of the Roaring Twenties. At the time, a number of American cars were frank imitators of Rolls-Royce. Earle put a different twist to that idea by borrowing heavily from another famous European luxury car, the Hispano-Suiza.

The result was a series of automobiles which many believe to be the most handsome Cadillac ever built. The color and style of the era is captured in John M. Walton's 1929 341 B Roadster, here photographed in New Orleans' French Quarter. Its 341 cubic inch V-8 engine produced 95 hp. Although it is not known exactly how many roadsters were made in that year, only seven are believed to have survived.

Startled would be the word to describe the reaction of the automotive world when the new Cord was introduced in 1935. Here was a car shockingly different, yet head-turning handsome. The design started out in 1934, intended as a lower-priced Duesenberg, but the project was put on ice and later revived and developed into the new Cord. It was imperative to show the car at the 1935 auto show in New York, but in order to qualify, 100 cars had to be built. Full-scale production could not be started—time was too short—and the 100 cars had to be assembled by hand. The transmissions did not arrive in time, so the showcars were not even running. But nothing could prevent the Cord from becoming the star of the show!

The beauty of the Cord was more than skin-deep. It was the only American car in 1936 with front-wheel drive, which permitted a silhouette so low that seventeen years passed before a production car had a lower roofline. Unit body construction—before it was even called that—was another Cord feature. The 1936 Cords were designated Model 810. In 1937 came the 812. A supercharged version became available that year, increasing power output on the V-8 Lycoming engine from 125 hp to 175 hp.

The "Survivor" featured here is a 1937 Sportsman owned by Douglas R. Johnson of Wayne, New Jersey. Photographed with the car is its famous designer, Gordon M. Buehrig—reunited with his creation in New York.

CADILLAC 1929

CORD 1937

Howard Marmon entered the automobile field in 1902 with an air-cooled V-2. Just four years later he introduced America's first V-8, also air-cooled. But both the V-8 and the air-cooling were later discarded. A new car was brought to the nation's attention in a dramatic way when the Marmon Wasp won the first Indianapolis 500 in 1911. Big six-cylinder cars were the flagships of Marmon's fleet from 1911 until 1927 when a small straight-eight was announced. This engine powered the entire model line-up from then on.

But these smaller, less finely detailed cars were not the kind of vehicles to kindle Howard Marmon's interest. In 1926 he began work on a 16-cylinder car. It was shown in 1930, but production was delayed until the following year. The Marmon V-16, regarded by many as the most advanced engine of its time, won its creator a SAE gold medal in 1930 for the most notable achievement.

The 1933 Marmon V-16 featured here belongs to Ruth Dougherty of Indianapolis, Indiana. It was the last unit to come off the line before production was stopped in 1933, when Marmon went into receivership. The body design of the Marmon 16 was credited to Walter Dorwin Teague, although his son later claimed to have done the actual work. It is not known exactly how many cars were built, but estimates run from 385 to 500 units. Of the more unusual body style shown here, the convertible coupe, supposedly only 43 copies were built, and 7 are known to remain today. The cost in 1933 was $4975.

In all the tales of wheeling and dealing that make up the history of the automobile industry, perhaps no story of promotions and practices is more complex than that of New Era Motors, nominal manufacturer of the Ruxton. Nominal because they never had a factory of their own, relying on the production facilities of Moon and Kissel with disastrous results for all.

The car itself, radically low for its time and superbly engineered, was the culmination of a dream for engineer William Muller. He had long been gripped by the idea that front wheel drive could do the job best. As an engineer at Budd Body Company, he convinced management to finance a prototype. With the aid of promoter Archie Andrews and after several false starts, the new Ruxton was on the road in 1930, but by late 1931 the firm was already in receivership.

The Ruxton had a straight-eight 268 cubic inch Continental engine developing 150 hp. For $3195 the buyer could have a roadster body such as the one pictured here, which belongs to Walter Bellm of Sarasota, Florida. These bodies were built by Baker-Raulang in Cleveland, Ohio. Ruxton was the only car of its day to eliminate running boards.

Production figures are estimated to be between 300 and 500 cars. The majority were built in St. Louis at the Moon plant, with the balance coming from Kissel facilities in Hartford, Wisconsin. When those two firms shut down, there was no one left to build the Ruxton.

MARMON 1933

RUXTON 1930

Harry C. Stutz founded his company in 1911, just in time to enter one of his products in the first Indianapolis 500. The car finished 11th—impressive enough for the newcomer to earn itself a slogan, "The Car That Made Good in a Day". Its high performance reputation was secured by the "Bearcat" models built from 1914 until the early Twenties.

But Stutz also became known as a luxury automobile, noted for its progressive engineering. The heart of their cars was a straight-eight engine with an overhead camshaft. In 1929 a supercharger was added to boost performance. Their final masterpiece came in 1931 with the introduction of a 322 cubic inch engine boasting dual overhead camshafts and four valves per cylinder. The model, designated DV-32, was very fast, fully the equal of 12 and 16-cylinder competition. Bearcats with the same power plant were guaranteed to exceed 100 mph, and the 9-main bearing engine was conservatively rated at 156 hp.

The 1932 Stutz DV-32 featured here belongs to Bruce McBroom of Hollywood, California, and is one of the few still in the hands of the original owner's family. Only approximately 55 cars were built of this model; the Stutz factory went bankrupt in 1935, and production facilities closed for good in 1937. This "Survivor" was photographed together with a vintage biplane at Santa Paula Airport. The two made a fitting pair. They symbolized a bygone era of fun and freedom on the ground and in the sky.

Warren, Ohio, was the 1899 birthplace of the Packard automobile. After a 1903 move to Detroit, Packard went on to become a leader in the luxury car field. Brilliant Chief Engineer Jesse Vincent and his crew came up with one pace-setting feature after another, such as the steering wheel and the H-pattern shifting layout. Packard was also one of the first to feature four-wheel brakes and the straight-eight engine. Although Packard made six-cylinder engines as well as a magnificent V-12, the smooth and superbly powerful straight-eight was the mainstay of Packard powerplants from 1924 through 1954.

It was only natural that Packard became the favorite car of Hollywood's elite. Howard Darrin had located his shop and showroom on Sunset Boulevard, and with the experience he had gained as a bodybuilder in Paris, he was exceptionally well equipped to design a model that would capture the imagination of this special clientele. The first cars were built in his shop, but when demand increased overwhelmingly, the Packard factory took over production in 1941.

The Packard Darrin featured here, owned by Maurice C. Wilson of Alameda, California, is representative of this 1941 line of cars which offered the refined combination of styling flamboyance and engineering excellence. These automobiles were faster and handled better than any other American competitor. Horsepower of the 365 cubic inch straight-eight was rated at 160. The car weighed a shade over 4000 pounds and carried a factory price of $4595.

STUTZ 1932

PACKARD 1941

The end of the Civil War coincided with the birth of a new firm organized to produce such essentials as bathtubs and birdcages. Later, production shifted to bicycle manufacturing, and then to products for which the firm is better remembered—automobiles of superlative quality. Their first car, the Pierce-Motorette, appeared on the streets in 1901. It was quickly supplanted by larger models, which soon became popular in the luxury automobile market. Pierce cars captured the Glidden Trophy four years in a row—a tribute to their dependable performance.

The fender-mounted headlights of the Pierce made it instantly recognizable day or night, and no other car had as distinctive an identity. That feature was used from 1914 until the last models rolled off the line. What could better represent Pierce-Arrow than the 1931 Convertible Town Cabriolet shown here? This magnificent ''Survivor'' belongs to Phil Hill, famous race driver and classic car restorer, and has been owned by his family since new. The car has a unique custom body created by Le Baron and built on a Model 41 chassis—the largest Pierce for that year—with an impressive 147-inch wheelbase. The 385 cubic inch straight-eight engine produced 132 hp at 3000 rpm.

Pierce-Arrow advertising matched the car in elegance. An ad from 1932 stated: ''The micrometer, not the clock, governs the building of each Pierce-Arrow''. Sadly, time was running out. The clock stopped in 1938.

''The last great introductory year—that is how many classic car enthusiasts remember 1931. It was the year Marmon brought out its V-16, and Cadillac its V-12. The Reo Royale was new that year and so was the Stutz DV-32. A new car in every respect but name, the Chrysler Imperial of 1931 had a totally new chassis and a straight-eight engine instead of a six. And riding on the biggest of those chassis—the custom Imperial Series—were some of the longest and leanest bodies ever to grace an automobile.

In 1924, Walter Percy Chrysler had taken the shaky old Maxwell Company and pulled it straight out of the doldrums. The first model, named after the man in charge, was an instant success. Just two years later the Chrysler line ranged from the 4-cylinder ''58'' up to the six-cylinder Imperial ''80'', with prices starting at $845 and topping off at $3600 plus.

The company probably waited too long to introduce their eight, but when they did it was a show-stopper. The LeBaron Roadster, such as the one owned by William F. Harrah, founder of Harrah's Automobile Museum in Reno, Nevada, bested the competition in every measure. At 145 inches, its wheelbase was longer by 5 inches than Packard's 840; Cadillac was bested by 11 inches. Under the hood the Chrysler generated 125 hp, five more than Packard or Lincoln and 30 more than Cadillac.

PIERCE-ARROW 1931

CHRYSLER 1931

Herbert H. Franklin had very definite ideas on how to engineer an automobile, particularly the cooling, and once he had made up his mind, he stayed with the concept. In 1902 he established a company in Syracuse, New York, and began manufacturing air-cooled cars. At that time he was one of several manufacturers who did so. But competitors would whisper that air-cooled automobiles overheated in hot weather. Franklin replied by padlocking a car in second gear and sending it off to churn the sands of the Mojave Desert or Death Valley. It seems fitting that many of the surviving Franklins are today found in the heart of desert country, like the 1931 Dual Cowl Phaeton pictured here. It belongs to Thomas H. Hubbard of Tucson, Arizona, and has a one-of-a-kind body built by Merrimac. The six-cylinder engine inside provided maximum power of 100 hp when new. In addition, Franklin advocated a "scientific light-weight" formula, which called for flexible frames of laminated wood and steel.

But when production ended in 1934, his cars had been the only air-cooled ones on the market for the last ten years. While the trend among makers of luxury cars shifted towards larger, heavier models that used rigid frames and water-cooled systems, Franklin stuck with his designs. Did air-cooling, flexible frames and full-elliptic springs really work? Famous long-distance record setter Cannonball Baker had this to say about the Franklin: "It was the most pleasant car to drive of any I ever handled."

Edsel Ford had a new car delivered to him when he was on vacation in Florida—a one-of-a-kind, built to his specifications. The year was 1939. The car, a Lincoln Zephyr. But it was no ordinary Zephyr. The body had been stretched, and lowered, and looked elegantly clean in design. So great was the appeal of its beauty that when Edsel Ford returned from vacation, he had 200 orders for the automobile—a car not even intended for production.

By the end of 1939, the Continental began to roll off the assembly line. They were all 1940 models and part of the Lincoln Zephyr series. Only 404 of these were built in 1940. The car featured here, owned by Robert F. Allen of Charlotte, North Carolina, is from that first run.

The Continental featured the very last V-12 to be used in an American car. Pistons were small—the engine displacement was only 292 cubic inches. The engine produced 130 hp at 3600 rpm. A look under the hood revealed a finely detailed piece of machinery. Valve covers and manifold were polished aluminum with chromed acorn nuts holding down the covers. The interior was not less refined in appearance: gold macoid fittings and a combination of leather and whipcord was normally used. Mr. Allen's car is an exception, being the only one delivered with all whipcord upholstery.

The Continental name survives today, but in truth there was only one Continental—a zephyr of freshness on the automotive scene.

FRANKLIN 1931

LINCOLN 1940

Devoting their lives to the creation, preservation and racing of automobiles, the three men pictured on this spread stand out as giants in their respective fields. To the left is Gordon M. Buehrig with one of his most acclaimed designs, the Cord. His career began early; at the age of 24 he was already chief designer for Stutz and a year later he took up the same position with Duesenberg. He continued to work for the Cord Corporation through most of the Thirties, creating another of his masterpieces, the 851 Auburn Speedster. To the right, William F. Harrah enters his 1931 Chrysler Imperial. Started in 1948 with a 1911 Maxwell, Harrah's Automobile Collection has grown to be the world's largest, including over 1500 vehicles: more than 350,000 visitors a year view the 1100 cars on display in Reno, Nevada. In the picture below, Phil Hill mounts one of the many classics in his garage, the 1931 Pierce-Arrow. This car belonged to the family since new and the first laps around the block as a teenager whetted his appetite for fast driving. His career as a race driver has taken him to all the famous circuits around the world and finally, as a crowning act, brought him the Formula One World Championship in 1961. Mr. Hill today spends all his time on restoration of classic cars, and is often seen driving them in his winning style at historic automobile races.

When Stutz introduced their new twin-camshaft engine, they chose to designate the dual valve version DV-32, referring to the total number of valves in the powerplant. The competition already enjoyed considerable success with their V-8's, V-12's and V-16's, and Stutz wanted to capitalize on the popularity of the V series. It was no coincidence, therefore, that the letter V and the number 32 were prominently displayed in the new emblem, as seen in the photograph to the right. The experts were, of course, not fooled but there was many a young car enthusiast who now believed that the V-32 era had arrived. Pictured further to the right is the center portion of the steering wheel belonging to the 1940 Continental. Based on the Lincoln Zephyr, and also marketed as part of the Zephyr line, it used the standard Lincoln Zephyr wheel. The emblem is an example of how long the Art Deco style influenced design—in the early Forties the peak of this art style was a decade in the past. The Packard insignia was used in company advertising as early as 1904. The picture to the right shows how it appears on the rear bumper of the 1941 Darrin. In those days it was common to base the company's logotype on the founding father's signature—in this case that of James Ward Packard. The Marmon 16 emblem was the work of Walter Dorwin Teague Associates. Although this studio was credited with the styling of the entire car, Mr. Teague's young son, who had not yet joined the organization was the actual designer. In fact the octagon theme incorporated in the emblem and other places was the father's main contribution to the styling. The picture captures the emblem applied to one of the hubcaps. Except for a small plaque on the dashboard, these were the only locations carrying the Marmon 16 identification.

Headlights were distinctive features on the classic automobiles. However, it is not evident to the casual viewer that many car manufacturers used the same few suppliers for their lights. Duesenberg, Stutz and Packard, for instance, utilized the same reflectors, but specified different lenses and mouldings in order to exhibit individuality in design. The large picture to the left shows what Auburn's styling department came up with for their 1931-32 models. The vertical bracket dividing the light, probably inspired by the recuperateur in Marchal lamps, was a design theme carried through on the small lights beside the windshield as well as on the grill itself. The oval headlights in the picture above belong to Marmon V-16. They were manufactured by C. M. Hall exclusively for Marmon and Reo. The small photograph to the far left, capturing the Packard tail light, shows the direction styling had taken by the early Forties. Gone was the flat glass on the round ball protruding on a stem, away from the fender. Instead, the light was now attached directly to the body, and the lens cover was molded to incorporate new ideas in function and design.

A colorful sunset creates a romantic mood for the soaring Franklin bird. It was given an airplane look to emphasize the parallel between the Franklin's aircooling and the aircooling used in aviation engineering. The Stutz radiator was crowned by the youthful features of the Egyptian sun god, Ra, with the asp on his forehead symbolizing power. The Pierce-Arrow ornament had its head cast separately from the body to insure perfect reproduction of the fine details of face and hair. The photograph above features the Continental's hood ornament with its new styling concept—now it combined beauty with utility as a hood release handle.

Some of the outstanding engineering triumphs of the classic era are featured on this spread. When a Duesenberg engine was developed for legendary race driver Ab Jenkins, it was discovered that a "ram's horn" induction system increased performance from 320 hp to 400 hp. This system was used on the SSJ once owned by Clark Gable. The impressive engine compartment is captured in the photograph on the left-hand page. The Marmon V-16 engine, in the small picture above, was a valve-in-head design like the early Cadillac V-16, but Marmon exploited this feature by employing cross-flow heads, with the induction system in the 45 degree vee and the exhaust manifolds on the outside. The engine was designed for light weight, and used aluminum castings extensively; the cylinders were formed by wet liners. The photograph above shows the Stutz DV-32 engine in all its polished beauty. The early straight-eight Stutz engines had a single overhead camshaft and only sixteen valves. When competing, for instance at Le Mans, this engine could not hold its own against the 4½ litre Bentley which had much less piston area but four valves in each of its four cylinders. The engine was then redesigned along pure racing lines, with twin camshafts and dual valve heads, making the DV-32 one of the fastest machines on the road.

Equipped not only with the obligatory speedometer and tachometer, but also a chronometer, the dashboard (in the photograph to the left) of Clark Gable's Duesenberg SSJ looks impressive. But in addition, the engine-turned steel dash also included an altimeter not shown in the picture but located to the right of the oil pressure gauge. The small photograph to the right shows another Duesenberg feature: one of the exterior exhaust pipes with its steel sheathing. In the early days of motoring, before sheathing was used and the pipes were left exposed, their red-hot glow was a beautiful sight in the dark, but they were obviously hazardous to come near. The 1931 Pierce-Arrow was one of the few cars to feature a mirror mount and a spare wheel holder combined into one unit—a minor detail but a very decorative one as can be seen in the photograph to the far right. The leather seat of the Marmon 16, in the picture below, is an example of the quality and craftsmanship of the classic era. True, the leather has some cracks but it is still in remarkably good condition after nearly forty years of wear.

Ballooning chrome surfaces of a Cord hubcap reflect the Manhattan skyline in the photograph on this page. The large cap, covering the entire steel wheel, came as standard on the Cord, and was one of the many innovations on this model. The prototype was tested with hubcaps lacking the holes, but when it was discovered that the brakes had a tendency to overheat, the holes were incorporated. Again, form was dictated by function, as in many styling decisions on the Cord. The hubs on the right-hand page belong to Stutz, Cadillac and Duesenberg. The Stutz hubcap, with its decorative cloisonné enamel work, hides a hub with five lug nuts instead of the center-lock hub used by Cadillac and Duesenberg, who, incidentally, had chosen the same supplier for their wheels. Both of these cars were originally fitted with painted wire wheels. The Duesenberg had a protective steel cover over the spokes, which was later removed and the wheels chromed for a more glamorous appearance. The Stutz was delivered with the chromed wheels, an option chosen by the owner, for which luxury he had to pay an additional $150.

Automobile enthusiasts of yesterday were exposed to the elements of nature in a way we do not experience today. Sometimes this was pleasant—who can not imagine the refreshing breeze of cool wind on a hot summer day. The photographs on this spread show three different body styles common for classic cars. None of them offered the traveler much protection. In the picture above, owner Al Ferrara occupies the sporty cockpit of Clark Gable's Duesenberg Roadster. This car had a light top with side curtains. Unfortunately, a case of claustrophobia could be provoked when top and curtains were used—the cockpit was narrow and the windows small. To the right, owner John Walton tries out the rumble seat of his 1929 Cadillac Roadster. This was a drafty but sought-after position from which to enjoy a Sunday afternoon drive. A definite problem was the lack of overhead protection—the sight of rain clouds on the horizon could spoil the fun. One way to approach the draft problem is shown in the photograph to the far right featuring owner Tom Hubbard in his 1931 Franklin Dual Cowl Phaeton. The cowl behind the driver's seat housed a second windshield. On this one-of-a-kind Franklin it could be rolled up and down according to the passenger's wish. There were no side curtains so the traveler was still left out in the cold—a hardship willingly accepted.

A CAR FIT FOR THE KING

There was excitement in the air today. It had been there all morning. This didn't mean that the Southern California beaches had suddenly become any whiter. Or that the Los Angeles sun was any brighter than usual. Or that Hollywood was cracking in its seams because of another and bigger scandal among the inhabitants of the movie colony. To young Charles Cord it simply meant that he had managed to arrange a lunch date with the girl that had occupied his mind for a long time.

There was excitement in the air for another reason too. It had been announced that Clark Gable had bought the short-wheelbase Duesenberg. Only two had been made of this rare model. It was the fastest car on the road in 1935, and it had attracted considerable attention during the time it had been displayed in the showroom here at the Duesenberg dealership on Wilshire Boulevard. And now it had been sold to Clark Gable. Everyone was talking about it.

"Did you know that Clark Gable had bought the short wheelbase?"

"Do you think he is going to pick it up himself?"

"Is Clark Gable coming here?"

It had been like that all morning.

Charles walked out to the garage where the Duesenberg was being prepared for delivery. He knew that his father, E. L. Cord, automotive wizard and the driving force behind the Auburn, Cord, and Duesenberg successes, must be pleased to have the

car sold to a celebrity like Clark Gable. It will make headlines, he thought. Charles almost wished he himself had been the salesman to make the deal. His father had sent him here to the Los Angeles dealership so he could gain firsthand experience of automobile sales procedures. It was part of a plan to make the son and heir familiar with the many different operations within the large Cord Corporation. After this he was supposed to move to the factory that made the Stinson airplanes.

The two men preparing the Duesenberg were almost finished. The hood was still off, leaving the gigantic powerplant fully visible. The polished aluminum parts and the green engine block made for a beautifully detailed piece of machinery. It was ex-

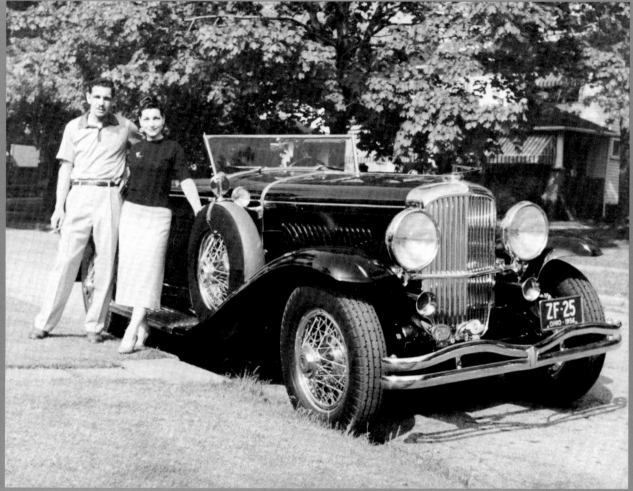

tremely powerful looking with the two ramshorn manifolds curving out from one side and the four exhaust pipes from the other. The white-wall tires on seventeen inch rims were spotless, and the light brown, freshly polished paint job was speckled with a pattern of dark and light reflections.

"Charlie!" The sales manager came charging into the garage, but stopped abruptly when he discovered Charles. Almost shouting, he delivered his message in a nervous, high-pitched voice: "We just had a call from MGM. They want us to deliver the car on the set where Mister Gable is filming today. I want you to drive it over there."

"I'm sorry, sir, but I have a date with my girl-friend. I just can't do it."

"Nonsense, Charles! You call her up right now and tell her you can't see her. This is important. You are the boss's son, you know, and there will be photog-raphers and reporters all over the place. This is public relations, you know what I mean?"

"Sure, sir. But. . . ."

"Charlie, I will not discuss this. Do it!" The manager stuck a hand into his vest pocket, found his watch, flipped the lid open, looked at it and then added: "You'd better get her started. We don't want to keep Mister Gable waiting, do we?"

"No, sir!" There was nothing he could do about it. He hurried back to the showroom, called his girl-friend, and then hurried back to the garage where the Duesenberg, in the meantime, had been started and was now idling with a deep rumble thundering from the exhaust pipes.

Charles drove up Wilshire Boulevard. When he noticed what a traffic-stopper the beautiful automo-bile was, he decided to avoid much of the lunch-hour rush by turning off on La Brea. It was an exciting experience to drive this Duesenberg. Charles felt the difference in power between this car and the other Duesenbergs he had driven. They normally had around 260 hp, while this one produced 400. He leaned forward and reached under the seat for the lever that regulated the exhaust bypass. He turned it and the sound behind him became violently louder, as the exhaust gases shot out unhindered. He drove like that until he realized that he was again attracting *(Continued overleaf)*

When Clark Gable took delivery of his second Duesenberg in the fall of 1935, his romance with Carole Lombard had not yet begun. But just a few months later their love was in full flame. Gable is shown with his first Duesenberg in the photograph to the right. Both cars played important roles, as they provided the elusive couple means to escape curious reporters. The present owner of the Gable car, Al Ferrara, is pictured above in 1956 with his wife Francesca. Al was often told that he looked like Gable, and a glance at the photograph confirms the striking likeness.

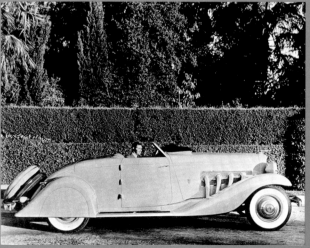

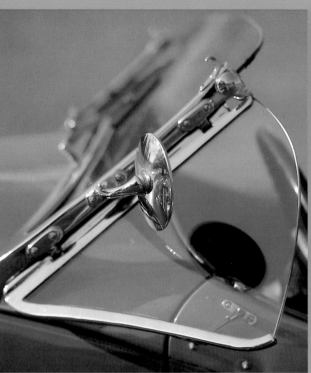

Film hero Clark Gable was the original owner of this sporty 1936 Duesenberg. The model had a shortened wheelbase and was capable of more than 130 mph. Only two of them were made, the first one ordered by another of Hollywood's "fast-car-lovers", Gary Cooper. The car featured here is the one Gable drove to the Mayfair Ball on January 25, 1936, when he fled the party with Carole Lombard and took her for a nocturnal drive around Hollywood. This came to be the starting point of the famous romance. The Duesenberg was photographed outside Cleveland, where present owner Al Ferrara keeps it in a condition worthy of its glamorous past. The distinctive form of the radiator, the windshield with its beautifully shaped windwings, the shrouded curves of the exhaustpipes, the stylized simplicity of the radiator ornament, all contribute to the timeless elegance that made Duesenberg the ideal of every car enthusiast.

too much attention, and reset the lever. When he reached Washington, he turned right and continued on that street until he saw the main building of Metro Goldyn Mayer.

He was met at the gate by a public relations agent from the studio. The man jumped up on the running board and proceeded to direct him through the labyrinth of studio lots, energetically pointing this way and that, until they arrived at an area opposite Stages Five and Six. He said Mister Gable's dressing room was just above the schoolhouse and that the last scenes for "Mutiny on the Bounty" had been filmed today. A crowd of reporters, photographers and studio personnel had already gathered on the street between the big sets.

The next thing he knew, "The King" himself was coming down the stairs from his dressing room. He was still wearing costume and make-up. In his white sailorshirt, open at the chest and wide at the wrists, and dressed in knee-length pants and socks, he looked out of place with the Duesenberg and the people gathered around it. The cameras clicked, and the famous smile flashed, and everyone crowded around the star as he slowly made his way to the car. Charles thought the famous actor looked different somehow, and suddenly he realized that the obligatory mustache had been shaved off for this role. Charles would later remember how he had handed over the keys to Mister Gable in a symbolic gesture for the photographers, and how they had shaken hands smiling at the cameras. People were crawling like ants over a just-captured bug, and Charles decided to leave as soon as possible. Everything was very tumultuous.

One day in the spring of 1936, a few months after the Duesenberg had been sold to Clark Gable, young Alfredo Ferrara drove his father's black Oldsmobile Sedan from Cleveland Heights, Ohio, where he lived with his parents, to a small neighboring town. Alfredo had come over from Messina, Sicily, at the age of seven. That was ten years earlier. Today he was going to see a girl he hoped would someday become his wife. He had met Francesca Epolito at a wedding some months ago, and had not been able to forget her. This time he was bringing Cannoli—the pastry

with cheese stuffing that she loved—and he was planning to ask her parents if he could take Francesca to the movies. After much pleading with her father, she won out, and the young couple was on their way to the theater. That first evening together they saw "Mutiny on the Bounty" with Clark Gable.

In 1947 Clark Gable sold the Duesenberg to George Stoll, the musical director of MGM. Stoll had the sheet metal sand-blasted and repainted a light beige. The brightwork was replated and the interior reupholstered in natural tan calfskin. Stoll had just completed the restoration when he decided to sell it to John Troka. The price was $2,500. Troka resold it from his shop in Chicago to the first big postwar car collector, D. Cameron Peck. When Peck broke up his collection in 1951, the Duesenberg was purchased by Perry Egbert of Attica, New York. Some years later, Egbert received a phone call from a man who was very eager to purchase the Gable car. A price was agreed upon over the phone and arrangements made for delivery to Cleveland. The new owner was Alfredo Ferrara.

The small photograph immediately to the left shows the Gable Duesenberg after the subsequent owner, George Stolle, was finished with its first restoration. Among other details, it included a repainting. The rest of the pictures on these pages show the magnificent machine in 1940, when it was still in Gable's possession. The cameraman was a young car enthusiast by the name of Strother MacMinn. He managed to get into Bob Robert's shop in Hollywood and with his Argus box camera captured these frames of the Duesenberg being tuned up. MacMinn today is a distinguished automotive historian and designer.

AUBURN

SENTIMENTAL JOURNEY WITH AN OLD FRIEND

It was Friday morning, August 11, 1972. John Keys woke up around ten, dressed and went out to start the Auburn. This had been his daily routine ever since he had retired from the Army and moved to Santa Barbara nine years earlier. He lifted the garage door and, at the familiar sight of the Auburn's hood emerging fully as the door opened all the way up, he felt a slight pain in his chest. He sat down behind the wheel, placed the key in the ignition lock, pulled out the choke and pressed the accelerator. The engine turned over but did not start. He pushed the accelerator pedal a little farther and then it fired. When he heard the familiar sound of the straight-eight settling down to a calm idle, he again felt the sensation in his chest. He went back inside the house to pick up his windbreaker and headgear. He would need them since he always drove with the top down. He eased carefully out of the garage and then accelerated up the street, pressing his hat further down on his forehead as the speed-wind increased.

John turned left on Modoc Street and right on Las Palmas Drive. It would take him through Hope Ranch and all the way down to the ocean. He enjoyed the early morning with its cool freshness, and he enjoyed the sight of the long rows of majestic palm trees lining both sides of the road. He glanced at the gauges on the dashboard. The water temperature was not yet up to what it should be, but everything else looked normal. He passed the golf course

and the lake on the left and was soon in the wooded area where the road curved in and out among the oak trees. Their long branches reached across the road, forming tunnels, and when he drove through them he leaned back and looked up, enjoying the sight of the branches rushing by silhouetted against the blue sky high above.

John spent much time thinking about the past, and on a clear morning like this it was easy to remember. I have had this Auburn for a very long time, he thought to himself. Let me think, she must be forty years old now because I bought her in 1932. It was on May 28, I remember. I must have wanted this old junkpile pretty bad, he thought. Ever since I first saw a Bottail Speedster I wanted one. And then I happened to see that ad in the newspaper announcing the bankruptcy sale in St. Louis, Missouri. I must have been crazy, he thought laughingly. I drove from Dupo, Illinois, the evening before the sale and slept all night in my 1928 Ford parked in front of the showroom. Every time I woke up during the night I looked out at the Auburn sitting there on the showroom floor bathed in bright lights. I wanted to be sure I was first in line the next morning. And I was! I got the Auburn for $900, which was just about half of what they normally cost. It was a very good deal I made, he thought to himself. But I really didn't have the money to do it, because I couldn't even afford to drive her for the next two years. I put her up on blocks and started her every day to keep the engine in shape.

Making a sharp left hand turn distracted him from his thoughts. He had entered the curve a little too fast and now had to brake and force the car back to the right side of the road.

When he came out of the turn he saw the ocean between the trees to the right. There were two more sharp turns, and then he was by the shore. He parked and turned off the engine and listened to the sound of the surf rolling up on the sandy beach a hundred feet below. He noticed a few sails out on the Pacific, and right in front of him he could see the Channel Islands. They had the same blue color as the ocean, but a stripe of white fog marked the division between sea and land. He started the car and continued driving along the coast, and he observed more sails the closer he came to the harbor.

In 1934 I had more money again. We were all doing a little better by then, he thought to himself and remembered the hardships of the Depression years. I was able to drive the Auburn at last. I was the coach for the high school football team, and sometimes I would drive around to other games to spy on rival teams, trying to figure out their tactics and crack their signal codes. Yes, those were the good old days, he thought to himself. But when the war came I had to put the Auburn on blocks again. Let me think; I joined the army in 1943 and went to Texas and then to Virginia, I believe, and then to Georgia, Washington, Michigan, California and finally ended up in Manila. I came back in 1946 and stayed in San Francisco and drove the Auburn there for six months until I was sent back to Manila. Then she was put up on blocks again.

He was still driving along the coast, but the shore and the road had changed directions, and he was now heading towards downtown Santa Barbara and facing the hills behind. He had a magnificent view of the city and the bay. Looking to the east, he could see the destination of his morning drive, the old Stearns Wharf Pier, where he expected to find his fishing-buddies.

It was in Manila that I met Lillian for the first time. She was a physical therapist at the Army hospital there. I had a jeep, and we used to go to Subic Bay and Corregidor Island to swim and lie in the sun on our days off. Then I was transferred back to the States, and moved the Auburn to Battle Creek, Michigan. It took several years before I met Lillian again. I was stationed in San Francisco and drove down to Santa Barbara in the Auburn. That's when Lillian saw her for the first time. Then we decided to get married and drove to Las Vegas for the ceremony.

In 1955 it was time to put the Auburn on blocks again. I left her with friends in Arizona while Lillian and I went to Heidelberg, Germany. We were there for five years, and then I was transferred to El Paso, Texas. We stayed there until I retired in 1963. It was a lot of moving around, he remembered, but the Auburn was always with me or waiting for me when I got back from those far-away places. You rusty old junkpile, he thought, I just can't seem to get rid of you.

(Continued overleaf)

Auburn owner John J. Keys was a keen fisherman. Here he is seen proudly displaying his catch while the boat makes its way home through San Francisco's Golden Gate. The picture to the lower left shows the Auburn in Michigan just after John returned from Manila where he served during the Second World War. To the right, the car appears in San Francisco. The year was 1951, and by now John was married. His wife, Lillian, is barely visible behind the windscreen. The Auburn in these photos was painted in a striking cream-and-red color combination. In the picture above, John poses in full uniform beside his prize possession, now repainted in black.

Boat-tail and fishing were factors that determined the choice of picture-location for this 1932 Auburn. The worn planking in the photographs covers the old pier at Stearns Wharf in Santa Barbara. This was the favorite fishing spot of Auburn-owner John J. Keys. A long career in the army took him all over the nation. When it became time to retire, he decided to settle down in Santa Barbara. The Auburn, which he had purchased new in 1932 for 900 dollars from a bankrupt Missouri dealer, went with him wherever he moved. He changed the color combinations on the car as often as he changed homesteads, but the characteristic lines of the boat-tail Auburn remained the same, drawing admiring attention wherever he went. Mr. Keys always worked on the Auburn himself, doing a little bit of engine repair, a little bit of upholstering, a little bit of painting. . . . The car today carries the traces of his loving care. There are fittings that do not work and there are rust spots—but what can you expect from a car that was driven almost every day for almost fifty years?

The road was curving east now, and he passed the marina with its forest of masts and continued out on Cabrillo Boulevard with all the motels on one side and the shore on the other. The beach was full of sunbathers. There were people walking on the sidewalks and sitting on the concrete wall along the playa. Some turned their heads and smiled at the sight of the old automobile, and others waved. He always waved back.

She looked good in red, he thought to himself, and she looked pretty nice in silver too. When she was new she was a dark green. When I got tired of that, I painted her beige and then red and then silver and then cream with red stripes. That was when we lived in San Francisco. I always felt that combination was too flashy, he told himself. That's why I decided to paint her black. Lillian and I had a terrible job getting all those layers of paint off. We worked hard for many months with razor blades and sandpaper. Then I sprayed her black. I like her in black, he decided.

The old planking of the pier protested under the Auburn's weight. John turned right after passing the restaurants and shops out there and continued on the western finger of the pier. He parked behind the last building and walked the rest of the way out to the small shack where the red triangle was hoisted. Two of his fishing-buddies were there, and they had seen him come.

"Aren't you fishing, John?"

"No, I don't feel too good today. Something in my chest. Are they biting?"

Everett made a face indicating disappointment as he pointed down in the yellow bucket by his feet. It was half filled with water, and two six-inch perch and one small halibut floated lifelessly in the bottom. Just then Albert started to wind up his line.

"I have one on, I think!"

"Don't let it jerk you into the water!"

John smiled, and Everett gave him a jab with his elbow. Albert reeled it in now with excitement on his face, and finally a small perch emerged from the muddy green water. The fish glittered like silver on the pier. It jumped for its life and slapped its tail against the planking.

"A real tap dancer, isn't he?"

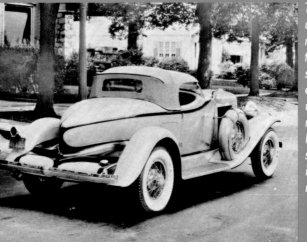

The new Auburn Speedster for 1932 is featured in the unique picture above, taken outside the factory showroom in Auburn, Indiana. Its designer, Al Leamy, is the proud gentleman behind the wheel. To the left a street scene from the Thirties focuses attention on the elegant tailend and the sporty top. The Speedster was used as an effective attention-getter in Auburn's promotion activities. Here the show has stopped outside Roosevelt Theatre in Chicago. Auburn's many racing successes helped create its fame. Here Wade Morton, in the picture to the right, is captured charging up the muddy finishing stretch at Pikes Peak in 1928.

John smiled again, and Everett helped to unhook the little fish and then threw it in the bucket. He wiped his hands on his pants and looked at John who stood close to the edge of the pier gazing down into the water where the mass of floating seaweed raised and sank with the surge of the waves.

"You don't feel good today, do you?"

"No, I think I'd better be on my way home. See you guys, maybe tomorrow. I'll give you a call. Maybe we'll go to Rincon Beach and fish off the rocks. Catch the big ones!"

When he returned to the car, he found a note on the windshield. It said, "Trade you for a 1949 Nash". He was used to getting messages like this. He didn't think much about them anymore. He started the Auburn and drove back. All the way home he didn't feel well, and when he arrived at the house he went straight to the couch and lay down. There was a sharp pain in his chest. Maybe it had been there all morning. But now it was stronger, and when Lillian came home he was very weak and he asked her to take him to the hospital. He thought of the new horn he had bought for the Auburn and the wood that he was working on for the top. There were so many things unfinished.

It was quiet when John was not around anymore. There was no activity in the garage. Neighbors helped Lillian put the Auburn up on blocks. She didn't feel like driving the car anymore, but she did start it every morning.

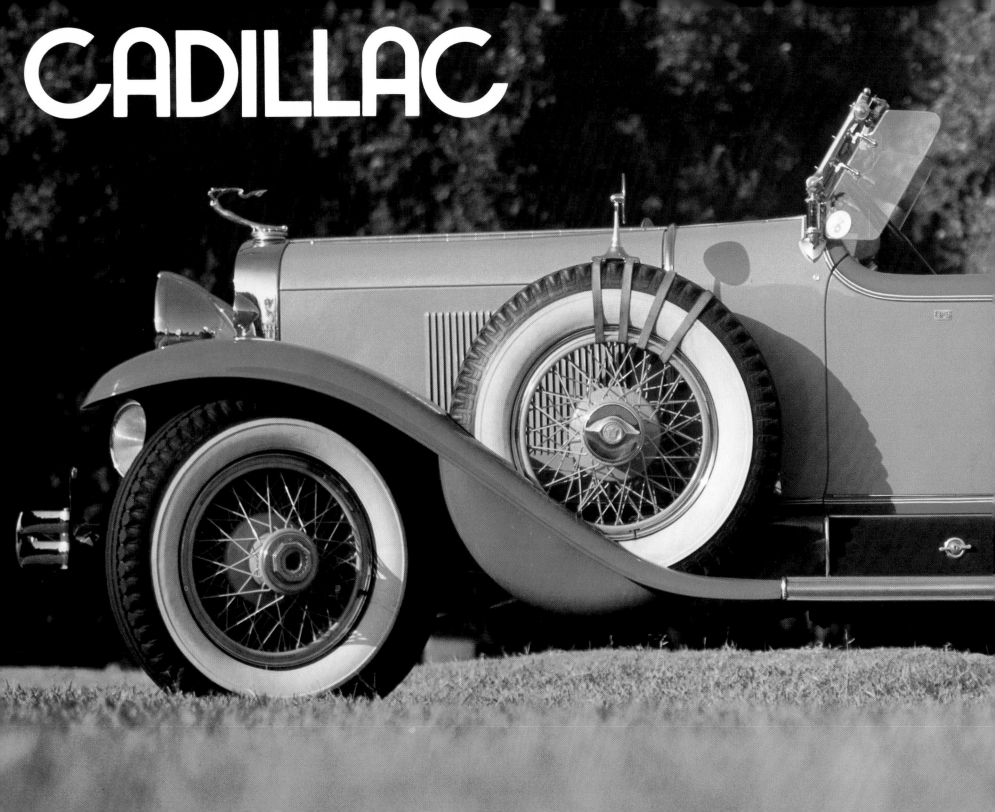

CADILLAC

DISCOVERY IN THE SWAMPLANDS

A Mercury station wagon cut through the early morning mist at a fast, steady clip. The two men inside sat silent and dozing. They were lulled by the monotonous singing of the tires on the road and the soft silhouette of the landscape that moved rapidly by. Thick fog lay like a blanket over the swamp-land on either side. The long cones formed by the head-lights registered on whirling mist, which the light made opaque and difficult to see through.

It was duck-hunting season. The men had left New Orleans while it was still dark, going south on Highway 35 into the Mississippi Delta to an area where it had always been good hunting. In the back seat were the supplies for the weekend and two guns, a Smith and a Browning Automatic.

At that particular moment they turned off the highway on to a smaller side road, the headlights sweeping in a wide curve across the swamp, and John's eyes caught a sight that stirred him wide awake. He could swear he had seen the front of an old Cadillac. It had appeared there for a split second only. He turned eagerly to his friend behind the wheel.

"Andy, did you see that?"

"What? I can't see anything but fog!"

"There was an old Cadillac back there. Turn around if you can. I want to check it out."

Andy stopped the car and backed up. It was that gray time of morning just before sunrise and the light was faintly sifting through the fog, but they could see the dark outline of a shack and an old car beside it. In the bright light of the headlamps, the car was clearly visible. The two men jumped out and walked over to it.

"It's a Cadillac, just as I thought. A 1929, I believe." John walked around the car to see the body style.

"It's a roadster with a rumble seat. Very unusual. I've never seen one before. Let's stop on the way back and find the owner."

John had been interested in cars as long as he could remember. He often thought about his first car, a 1928 Ford Roadster and how he and three of his friends had driven it to the Chicago World's Fair in 1933. His sister Beverly had come along with them on the trip, and they had teased her about being their chaperone, making sure the four boys would not get into trouble. That was a long time ago.

The duck hunting went all right, but John kept thinking about the Cadillac. He wondered if it would be a good car to restore. He had been looking for a car like this one, a car that would be worth spending time and money on. A couple of hours before dark they decided to return, and on the way back they stopped to take a closer look at the Cadillac. John was pleased to find the owner home.

However, the car was in worse condition than he had thought when he first saw it. The cockpit was covered with gunny sacks. There was lumber stacked on top of it and under it on the ground. The car had been sprayed light blue and the layer of paint was very thin, looking like a prime coat. There were big, rusty holes in the running boards and fenders. The headlights had been pushed back into the radiator in an accident long ago. He noticed details like the right brake light. It was from a Chrysler. The other light was missing with just a broken bracket left.

It would be quite a task to restore the car, he thought to himself, but it would be possible. The more he thought about it the more excited he became, but he didn't want to let the owner know how he felt about the Cadillac. Instead, he pointed out the things that were wrong, and finally mentioned that he

thought $700 would be a fair price. The owner didn't seem too disappointed but said he would think about it and would call when he had decided.

When they got back in the station wagon Andy smiled and looked at John.

"Well, I think you just bought yourself a car!"

I met John Walton many years later. To be accurate, it was sixteen years after the episode in the Mississippi Delta. We were sitting on the veranda outside John's home in Metarie on the north side of New Orleans. We talked about the Cadillac. As we talked, we kept glancing at the car. It was parked in the driveway with the front wheels turned full tilt, and it looked very elegant in the late afternoon sun.

We talked about all the time and money he had put into the restoration of the Cadillac and how he had done it. After he picked it up from the Delta he had parked it in the garage to dry. Then he had taken it for a test drive to find out all that was wrong with it. The engine sounded bad and something was terribly wrong with the gear box. The shift lever went all
(Continued overleaf)

The pictures on this spread come directly from Cadillac owner John M. Walton's private photo album. To the far left John is mounting his Indian motorcycle. He had just turned sixteen and was thrilled with his new toy, purchased used from the local sheriff's department, and given to him by his father. Three years later, in 1933, he was ready for his first automobile, a 1928 Ford Roadster. His sister Beverly joins him in the picture to the left, where they pose in front of the Ford. John was always involved with machinery and in the photograph to the upper left, he is in the process of testing a Marmon engine. The snapshot above shows the Cadillac as it looked just rescued from a hurricane threatening to flood the Mississippi delta where John, a few months earlier, had discovered the rare survivor.

Sophisticated elegance surrounds this 1929 Cadillac resting in the courtyard of a New Orleans mansion. The dazzling "Survivor" looks like it had just rolled off the showroom floor—a striking contrast to the car's condition two decades ago, when owner John M. Walton discovered it rusting in a shack along the Mississippi River. Years of patient labor involving reconditioning of every detail and nationwide search for missing pieces, brought the Cadillac back part by part to its original splendor. Details like the instruments and mirror mount shown in the pictures above were hard enough to find, but the crowning radiator ornament proved nearly impossible to locate. It was finally found by a friend who happened to spot it attached to the front fender of a motorcycle. Captured in the photograph to the left, the radiator ornament becomes a symbol for all restorers—it portrays Diana, goddess of the chase.

the way up to the dashboard in one gear and in another it came all the way down to the seat. He recorded everything in a notebook so he would remember later on when the Cadillac was all taken apart.

After the test drive he began to dismantle the body. He took off the fenders, the wheels, the dashboard, the floor board and the running boards. When he lifted the windshield frame he found the original color underneath on the cowl. It had been black and green with white striping. He measured the width of the stripes and the distance between them. He wanted to repaint the striping, and he wanted it exactly the way it originally was.

And then there was the search for parts. Most of them he had found through contacts in the Cadillac Club. Others he had to make himself. But some he was very lucky with, like the clock on the dashboard. He found it in a 1930 Cadillac Sedan here in town. Another part that was hard to locate, but that he luckily acquired, was an original hood ornament. A friend spotted it attached to the front fender of an old motorcycle. It was just before Christmas, so the friend wrapped it and put it under the tree.

"That was the best gift that Christmas!" said John and laughed, wrinkling his tanned face.

"Did I tell you about the rats in the seats? No? When I took off the old worn leather I found that rats had made themselves comfortable in the cushions. It was quite a job to get all that cleaned out. They must have used it for years."

"It was also an interesting experience to pick up the Cadillac from the Delta. A few days after I had agreed to buy it, I heard on the news that there was a hurricane approaching. My first thought went to the Cadillac, of course. I had to get it out of there since the high water would flood the entire area and maybe even wash the car away. I asked my friends Andy and Ashton if they would help me. We took the station wagon and went down there Sunday morning."

"We didn't have any rain on the way down, but we could see it coming. The horizon was a dark blue-gray above the Gulf and we were afraid it would be over us before we could tie the Cadillac to the Mercury and be on our way back. We made it down, but on the way back we were caught in the worst rain

storm I can remember. Andy drove the station wagon and Ashton sat in the back of it with the rear window open so we could talk back and forth about the towing. I was driving the Cadillac. We had rigged up an old tarp over the top of the car but the wind and rain came down so hard on us that it was impossible to keep it in place. I was wet to the skin when I arrived home."

We both laughed and then we just sat there in silence looking at the Cadillac in the driveway. John had a distant expression in his eyes, as if all the hard times and all the good times he had experienced with the Cadillac were passing in review. I understood how he felt.

Elegance was the key word in classic car styling as well as in design of showroom displays. The photograph to the far left, from 1929, was taken in McAlister Brothers' showroom in Pittsburgh. Elegance is also reflected in the pictures of John M. Walton's Cadillac after its restoration. In the small picture to the far left the car is receiving last minute detailing before entering a car show. The other photographs were taken by a New Orleans newspaper for an article on the unique classic and its unusual story. Notice the lowered windshield in the picture to the left. This feature allowed a most sporty driving experience.

CONVERSATION ABOUT THE SHAPE OF A NOSE

"When I was here in New York in 1935 the traffic was almost as intense as it is today. Of course, many things have changed; the styling of the cars and their colors, for example. But there is another difference that I'm aware of if I close my eyes and listen. It's the sounds. The engines sounded different then. And the horns."

Manhattan was humid and hot like a boiling kettle. The steam rising from the culverts in the streets made it seem like the city was boiling even inside. The New Yorkers were rushing to their favorite restaurant for a quick lunch or to the drugstore for some small-item shopping or both. Gordon Buehrig and I were on our way to "Le Chanteclair", the famous restaurant operated by French prewar racing ace René Dreyfus, and a meeting place for people representing many different occupations and interests in the automotive world. We made our way through the crowded sidewalks heading west. We had just left the Waldorf-Astoria on Park and Lexington and were going to number eighteen on 49th Street. It was a short walk but a memorable one.

A few weeks earlier I had called Mister Buehrig in Grosse Point, Michigan, where he lives, and asked him if he would be willing to meet me in New York. I told him about my plans for photographing him alongside one of his masterpieces, the Cord. This milestone in automotive styling history had been introduced at the New York Auto Show in 1935. I felt it would be a nostalgic event for the designer to be reunited with his creation here in New York forty years later. Now he was here. And he remembered as we continued to walk:

"The show was held at the Commodore Hotel on Lexington Avenue. I had been sent there by the Cord Corporation as an observer, I guess. I was in New York for two days without anything to do. I had no official function. I was never part of any promotion activity. I was not invited to attend a press conference. I was never introduced as the designer. Can you believe that? It's not that I feel bitter. I've received my share of fame later in life, but I'm mentioning it as an illustration of what a designer was in those days— just some youngster in the styling department. Yet, it was the way the Cord looked that made it the sensation it was."

Passing Madison, we realized we had crossed on red and had to sprint to safety on the other side. Mister Buehrig chuckled to himself.

"Come to think of it, I did have a specific reason to go to the show. I was asked to bring the scale models of the Cord. Management had decided that they should be displayed there. They had been made for the initial presentation earlier in the year. For the New York show they had to be fixed up again. So we fashioned glass display-cases to protect them. Dale Cosper, Dick Robinson and Vince Gardner worked with me on the project. Like everything else on the Cord, it was done at the last minute. We finished around eleven in the evening, the night before the show opened. I remember going to bed immediately to get in a few hours of sleep before I started for New York at three in the morning. I had a donut and a glass of milk. Then I drove straight through. But the funny part was that I drove a hearse—an undertaker's service car actually. The Auburn people wanted to display it at the show. I put the models where the coffin was supposed to be. It all worked very well, but I caused a lot of commotion when I arrived at the show and unloaded my unexpected cargo."

It was difficult to continue conversation on the sidewalk. His sentences jumbled with words from passersby and got interrupted by accelerating buses and cars. I tried to find out where we were. I saw the canopy of "Le Chanteclair" before I discovered

number eighteen. Inside we were met by the usual noise of a busy restaurant, but here it was more subdued. The sounds of knives against plates and dishes being discretely cleared from the tables only aroused our appetites further.

When my eyes had adjusted to the soft lighting, I noticed that the room was very narrow up front where the bar was located. Car club emblems and portraits covered the walls on both sides. The old yellowing photographs and the modern color prints formed a mosaic of smiling racedrivers in winning poses with old-time goggles around their necks or carrying helmets with the new space-look in their hands. They were inscribed with flashy signatures and
(Continued overleaf)

Pictured to the left is Cord designer Gordon M. Buehrig behind his desk in the Auburn factory on South Main Street in Auburn, Indiana. The photograph was taken in 1934 while Mr. Buehrig was still working on the Cord design. His combined office and studio was located in a partitioned corner of the Engineering Department. Through the windows he could look out on the corn fields below. A collection of colored metal chips can be seen on the wall behind. These were used to select the different color combinations for the Cord. For his personal car, Mr. Buehrig chose "Cigarette Cream" with a red interior. The car is shown in the two pictures on the opposite page. They were taken in 1938 when Mr. Buehrig purchased his Phaeton from a Detroit dealer. The visual experience of driving the Cord was naturally pleasing to Mr. Buehrig, but the mechanical end of it gave him trouble. When the front joints gave out three years later, he decided to sell. Mr. Buehrig today is a popular guest at car shows and club meets. In the recent photograph above, he is seen in the cockpit of a Cord Beverly Sedan.

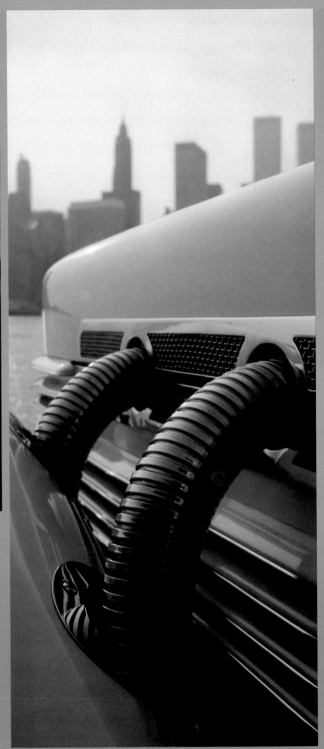

Skyscrapers form a monumental background to the Cord and its creator, Gordon Buehrig, in the double page picture on previous color spread. Car and designer are back together again in New York as they were in 1935 when the Cord was first introduced at the auto show. Buehrig's design was not only original in its general concept— no longer was there an air intake at the front of the hood—but also uninhibited in detail design—the curiously peering headlights were made to disappear. This feature, pictured to the far right, was also an automotive first.

personal messages. Further down, the room widened and took on a different atmosphere with softly painted murals from what must have been Paris as it looked before the war.

A finely built man in his late sixties came up to us. His hair was gray and thinning. The dark suit matched his cultured manners as he informed us that our table was not quite ready and would we please make ourselves comfortable at the bar for a few minutes. Mister Buehrig leaned closer to me and whispered as we mounted the bar stools.

"That was René Dreyfus himself!"

I turned around and looked at the man as he made his way between the tables. I was surprised. He seemed so refined. But, I thought to myself, there is no rule that says a racedriver has to be strong and violent. On the contrary. The cars themselves are strong and violent and it takes a sensitive body and mind to control them. Dreyfus had mastered the brutes of the Thirties—famous racecars like the Bugatti and Alfa-Romeo and Maserati. The man had certainly proved himself a racedriver of top class, I thought. I turned to Mister Buehrig. I wanted to lead the conversation back to him and the Cord. I asked him where he had found inspiration as a designer and who or what had influenced him. He hesitated a moment before answering.

"Well, I was an admirer of Le Corbusier and his concept of allowing form to follow function. I've always protested against the conventional form when function required a change. If you analyze the styling of the Cord you would be surprised to find that so little was dictated by esthetics alone. I have a good example for you. The area in front of the nose between the fenders was all flat and uninteresting in the original design. The transmission on the front-wheel drive Cord, as you already know, was ahead of the radiator, and when the vacuum shifting device was added on top of it, a styling problem was created. But I let it solve itself. We built a wooden mock-up of the area. Over this we placed strips of hot clay and smoothed it out. The resulting form was actually dictated by the mechanical components underneath, but I thought the esthetic effect was excellent."

Mister Dreyfus interrupted our conversation by

announcing that the table was ready. We followed him and before sitting down, I asked if he recognized the man in my company. He said he was not sure but thought the face was familiar. In spite of Mister Buehrig's protests, I proceeded to introduce him as the famous designer of the Cord. Mister Dreyfus lighted up and showed an expression of delight that only a Frenchman's face could exhibit.

"It is a great honor to have you as our guest. Please be seated. I will be back to talk more as soon as I have a moment."

My thoughts returned to the fascinating insight I had just received into the mind of one of the most accomplished automotive designers of all time. I asked him if the distinctive front of the Cord, with its wraparound louvers, also was a result of the form-follows-function theory. He nodded and drew with his finger on the tablecloth as he talked.

"You know, the Cord actually started out as a small Duesenberg. In the first design I incorporated one of my favorite concepts. I always felt that the engine compartment should be sealed to keep the engine clean and beautiful. In order to accomplish that, the airflow had to be kept out of the engine-area. I solved this by placing two radiators outside, one on each side between the wheels. This concept actually gave birth to the new look of the front since there was no longer a radiator to design around. The Duesenberg project was shelved, but when we later started on the new Cord these ideas were re-vived, and even though the sealed engine compart-ment and the two radiators were abandoned, a new look had been conceived. And all as a result of the desire to let form follow function."

Mister Dreyfus approached the table with a look of utmost reverence. He had a small silver tray in his hand, and balanced on the polished surface were three small glasses containing a golden-brown liquid. He set one glass down in front of Mister Buehrig, one in front of me, and lifted his own in a toast.

"May I present you with a glass of Grand Marnier. This is what we always drank when I was working in the Bugatti factory. A toast to the Cord!"

"To the Bugatti!" Mister Buehrig said.

"Santé", I said. I had always thought it sounded very French.

Rich and flamboyant Hollywood was a natural market for the Cord. In the picture to the left, a Phaeton is captured during a demonstration tour. Notice that only one of the headlights had been raised—getting the attention was the name of the game. The Cord in the photograph above is one of the first Sedans. This one had not yet been fitted with the standard hubcaps. The setting is E. L. Cord's Beverly Hills Estate. To the right, the first 1937 Model 812 is seen outside the Country Club in Auburn, Indiana. A sharp eye will discover that the bolts holding the plates around the exhaust pipes had not yet been moved inside.

MARMON

SEVENTY GRAND FOR THE GRAY SIXTEEN

William Ansted leaned back in the chair, placed his elbows on its padded armrests, folded his hands in front of himself and proceeded to stare thoughtfully at an insignificant spot on the opposite wall.

On his way to the factory that morning, his mind had been preoccupied with the analysis of certain developments that threatened the very existence of his company. He owned Metal Auto Products and manufactured fenders, splashpans, hoods and similar body details for Auburn, Stutz, Marmon and many other car makers. The factory was located on West Henry Street in Indianapolis, only four or five blocks north of the Marmon plant. William, or Bill, as everyone called him, had arrived late to the office. After going through the mail with his secretary, he was again alone with his thoughts.

He had been concerned about Marmon's financial situation for over a year now, and had lately became even more alarmed when he learned that they were discontinuing their eight-cylinder line and were only going to market the Sixteens. First of all, he felt Marmon had confused their public image by marketing cars in all price ranges. Their basic line of cars is by no means exciting from an engineering or styling viewpoint, but to rely only on the very exotic and expensive Sixteen is suicide, he thought. Secondly, he didn't believe the market for luxury cars existed anymore. Most people don't have that kind of money, he observed, and the few who have don't want to let it show.

The night before, unofficial sources confirmed that Marmon would, in fact, soon receive the final blow. I should have seen it coming, he reflected, and I should not have been so generous with their credit. I have to do something about it immediately, he decided.

Bill leaned forward, reached for the intercom and pressed the button marked "Accounting". A crackling noise signaled that someone was listening at the other end. He proceeded to give orders to have the unpaid Marmon invoices prepared.

"Add them all up and let me know as soon as you have the total!"

He leaned back in the chair again and sighed. I'm too young for these kinds of problems, he thought to himself. I'm only twenty-five and should be out looking for a wife. But I have always felt it my solemn duty to continue the family business, he thought and sighed again.

The Ansteds had been in the automotive industry for more than three decades. E. W. Ansted bought Ansted Spring and Axle Company in 1895. It became the largest manufacturer of automobile springs in the country. In 1908 the Ansted family had acquired Central Manufacturing Company. This firm supplied the bodies for most of the cars made in Little Detroit, Connersville, Indiana. The most well known of the family's ventures was the Lexington Motor Company, which E. W. Ansted had purchased in 1913. An unusually high level of quality could be maintained on the Lexington car because so many of the components were manufactured by the Ansted family's own companies. Racing successes added to the popularity of the Lexington and, during the 1921 model year, nearly 1,000 units were produced every month.

We were into just about everything that had to do with cars, Bill thought to himself. It was like a small empire, but then things began to happen, why, I'm not quite sure, he reflected. But maybe we grew too fast. In 1924 we had to sell the Spring and Axle Company. Two years later a Chicago Company bought the Lexington service inventory and the stock of completed cars. Later that same year, the Lexington plant was sold for 35,000 dollars. In 1928 the Cord Corporation purchased Central Manufacturing. A year later came the Wall Street crash, so I guess much of what happened to us had to do with the national economic situation. Yet in 1933, he reflected, we are still feeling the effects. It seems like almost

everyone had problems, and now Marmon's turn has come, he thought as the crackling intercom returned him to his present situation.

"Mister Ansted, the unpaid Marmon accounts add up to 70,000 dollars, Sir."

"70,000 dollars? Have all the invoices brought to my office immediately, please!"

The invoices arrived from the accounting department, and he stood up from his chair, placed the invoices in his case, grabbed his coat and went out. He had decided to go over to the Marmon people and talk to them.

Maybe I can get most of the money before the bottom falls out if I act immediately, he thought to himself as he started walking north. Just before entering the Marmon office building, he stopped for a moment in front of the showroom window. There was a shiny gray Sixteen on display, a Convertible Coupe. Very beautiful, he reflected, and then continued on to the office building and went upstairs.

The situation at the Marmon Company was worse than expected. There wasn't any cash available. He was offered some tooling equipment as partial payment, but it didn't amount to much. He became extremely depressed when he realized the extent of the loss his company would have to take.

Bill pleaded with them, but they had nothing useful to offer except the tools. He knew that very soon legal procedures against Marmon would start, and he realized that it was risky to come away with too much more than their other creditors. But suddenly an idea shot into his mind.

"How about the Convertible Coupe you have in the showroom window? I'd be willing to take the tooling and the car and write the rest off. What do you say?"

"It's the last one we have, and we planned to sell it and raise some cash for the payroll."

There was a brief pause.

"But if you agree to write everything off today, we will agree."

"Agreed then! Have the car removed from the showroom. I'll sign the papers and take the car with me right now. This has got to be the world's most expensive automobile!"

(Continued overleaf)

Original Marmon owner William B. Ansted was a cosponsor of the cars that won Indianapolis in 1964 and 1967. Here he is photographed with racedriver A. J. Foyt in front of the Lexington, an automobile once manufactured by the Ansteds. The pictures to the left and right show the Marmon possessed by James Rasmussen. He purchased the car in 1937 and kept it until 1955. To the right, Mr. Rasmussen and a friend try to solve a muffler problem they incurred during a trip to Lake Maxim Kuckee in northern Indiana. Notice the flared fenders, the hood vents and the spun wheel covers; all styling alterations executed by Mr. Ansted.

Returning to Indianapolis Motor Speedway, the Marmon V 16 in these pictures displays its innovative, yet classic lines. The large photograph to the right shows the wide valance of the front fenders. This unique styling feature was designed to cover "unsightly mechanical details" such as spring ends and shock absorbers. The slanted windshield and the similarly slanted radiator with its artistically sculptured form, were other innovations claimed to reduce wind resistance. The "Survivor" featured here was the last car to be completed before production was halted in 1933. A few years earlier, a stock Marmon V 16 had set a new speed record at Indianapolis. Circling the track for 24 hours, it reached an average speed of 76 mph. Almost fifty years later Marmon returns to the Speedway. The double-page picture on previous colorspread shows the car in Gasoline Alley—the legendary row of garages where so many famous racecars were prepared for the Indianapolis races, and where most certainly this Marmon had been parked before by its first owner, racing enthusiast and automotive manufacturer William B. Ansted. The photographs on this spread were taken on the lawn inside the oval. The old wooden grandstands, which still remain, are visible in the background of the picture to the far right.

Bill could finally manage a joke and felt relieved once an agreement had been reached. He also felt excited thinking of the magnificent automobile that would be waiting for him outside.

William Ansted kept the Marmon for almost four years. During that time he modernized it by adding new fenders with skirts. He also changed the side panels on the hood. The new ones had vents designed to resemble the latest models on the market. When this work was completed, the car was painted black. But these changes only helped for a few months. He wanted the latest, and traded the Marmon for a Cadillac.

In the fall of 1937 two young car enthusiasts, William and James Rasmussen, noticed the Marmon in a used car lot on the corner of Meridian and 16th Streets in Indianapolis. When they inquired about the price, they were quoted a sum of 500 dollars. William, the oldest of the brothers, was very persistent, and finally the salesman gave up and let it go for 175 dollars. A few months later, James became eighteen and managed to buy the Marmon from his brother. The automobile became his everyday transportation, which he used until the outbreak of the war, when gas rationing made it impractical to drive a car that only got five miles to a gallon. After the war the Marmon became more of a prestige vehicle, used only for special occasions like circling around town on New Year's eve with the top down. He always kept the car garaged and in good running condition, however. In 1955, John Hoggat offered 750 dollars for the Marmon. James needed the money and the space. The Marmon had a new owner again after eighteen years.

That same year, Jim Dougherty was working on his 1938 Pierce Arrow in his garage. There was something wrong with the fuel pump, and he wanted to investigate it. The tank was full, so when the fuel line was disconnected the gasoline started to spill on the ground. Jim put a washpan under the engine to catch it. Then he happened to come too near one of the battery terminals with his wrench, and a spark jumped the gap, igniting the gasoline in the washpan. Jim reacted quickly and moved it out from under the car. Just at that moment, it flamed up in his face,

and he threw it away in panic, spreading the burning gasoline all over. Jim barely managed to get out of the garage before it was enveloped in flames. He received third degree burns on his legs and minor burns on the rest of his body.

It was a sad day for Jim and his wife, Ruth, both classic car collectors. They were, of course, sad about Jim's injuries. But after all, they knew they would heal. The cars they had lost in the fire, on the other hand, were lost forever. Jim thought of the Pierce, the Packard, the convertible Maybach, the Rolls-Royce Towncar, the convertible Duesenberg and the other cars that now were totally destroyed, or only good for parts.

The one thing that kept Jim's spirit up was his plan for a new collection. Before the fire, he had heard of the Marmon Sixteen belonging to John Hoggat. Now he contacted John with an offer. John felt this was something he wanted to do for Jim and Ruth. After all, they had lost their entire collection. So the car got a new owner.

The leg burns healed very slowly, but the convalescence was shortened by a special project that Jim undertook. He had borrowed an original repair manual and was retyping it page for page. It took a long time, but it was a nice way to start over again. And he didn't think about the pain in his legs or the cars he had lost.

The Marmon Sixteen's powerplant was an engineering masterpiece. Its 200 hp would propel the unusually light car to 105 mph or more. Every car came with a written guarantee to that fact. Second owner James Rasmussen once reached 112 mph and maintained that unless a butterfly valve in the exhaust manifold had not stuck he would have reached an even higher speed. Shown above is the no-nonsense dashboard of the Sixteen. The instruments were set high, and this, together with the uncluttered design, gave better visibility than most cars of the day. An Arvin heater and a Motorola radio, both of the era and still in the car today, can be seen under the dashboard.

TO AWAKEN A SLEEPING BEAUTY

"Listen to this, Al. It's a newspaper clipping from 1929. It doesn't show the name of the paper, but the title of the article is 'Mystery Car'. It's hilarious! I have to read it to you."

The Ruxton was parked outside the restoration shop and Al was kneeling on the grass beside it. The hood panels were removed on both sides, revealing the straight-eight Continental engine inside. He was trying to figure out why it didn't start. I was sitting on a folding chair in front of the Ruxton, supposedly at work polishing the headlamps. But the Florida sun was hot on my back, and it made me lazy. Finally I threw the polishing rag on the grass and picked up the folder. It contained Ruxton memorabilia in the form of photographs, drawings and clippings. An enthusiast in New Orleans had sent it.

I thought the article was very amusing, and I just had to read it to Al in spite of the rapt expression on his face.

"I rode downtown yesterday morning in a new car—a front-wheel drive affair built so low to the ground that all the cars we passed seemed archaic. For the floor of this new car is as low as the transmission on most other cars—a trifle more than seven inches from the ground. There have been one or two makes of front drive trucks but this is the first passenger sedan of this type—and its low-slung body naturally attracted the attention of other drivers and, of course, the traffic cops. Whenever we were held up by traffic the heads of the drivers of cars nearby were stuck out like turtles and the policemen asked questions.

'What kind of car is this?' asked a Lafayette Street traffic cop, when we were stopped by the lights at Canal Street.

Pictured in the unique photographs on this page is William Muller, who in 1926 began to realize his engineering dream of a front-wheel drive automobile. In the picture above he is seen beside the first prototype. At this point it did not have a name, except for the nickname "Gator". Later a question mark was placed on the radiator, and it stayed there until the car was finally christened "Ruxton", after a wealthy banker. The prototype at this point carried the distinctive radiator, hood and fenders which would become Ruxton trademarks, but the design of the tailend had not been finalized yet. In the picture to the right, taken at the same time as the one above, William Muller has removed his hat and squeezed down behind the wheel of the prototype. Featured on the left-hand page is another unusual photograph. It shows promoter Archie Andrews' personal Ruxton Sedan outside his California residence in Altadena.

'A Zunkst,' its driver replied.

'Where is it made?' asked the cop who eyed it all over.

'In Czecho-Slovakia,' replied its driver.

'It's a new one on me,' admitted the officer, 'them Czechs must be clever fellows.' "

Al didn't even look up, or otherwise acknowledge that he had heard what I read to him. When I leaned over to find out what he was doing, I saw his scarred and oily fingers digging deep into the starter engine. The cigarette between his lips was short, and its smoke caused him to squint. He was too engrossed to even shake off the ashes.

I had arrived in Sarasota, Florida, the evening before, having driven straight through from Savannah, Georgia. In the morning I woke up early. I took a few laps in the pool at the Driftwood Motel, had my breakfast in the coffee-shop further down the street and went through my camera equipment to make sure everything was all right for the afternoon's shooting. After that, I left for Bellm's Cars and Music of Yesterday. It was a privately owned museum with an outstanding collection of music-machines. They also had quite a number of old cars. Among them, I had been told, a Ruxton.

I had called the museum in advance to explain to them about the book I was working on and to obtain permission to photograph the Ruxton. But before I let them know I was there, I wanted to see the car by myself first. I paid the entrance fee and began to look around. The lighting was dim, but there were spotlights arranged here and there, which focused on set decorations with life-size, costumed dolls placed around the cars. I noticed several classics. Right by the entrance was a Duesenberg Roadster; an L-29 Cord rested further down in the corner; and specially featured were a Packard and a Rolls-Royce, both formerly owned by Mister Ringling of the famous circus family. The collection looked like someone arranged it in this fashion many years before and had then left it alone. The years had improved the old-time atmosphere, but the condition of the cars had suffered.

I almost missed the Ruxton, squeezed in among the Fords and the Chevrolets as it was. I only noticed it (Continued overleaf)

Bright afternoon light illuminates the 1930 Ruxton casually parked on a deserted beach outside Sarasota, Florida. This rare "Survivor" was taken for a drive for the first time in nearly twenty-five years! The Ruxton was not only brilliantly engineered, achieving a low profile by means of front wheel drive, but also provocative in appearance, with its unusual fenders and radiator. The use of "Woodlite" headlights, pictured to the far left, gave the Ruxton an even more unique look. The emblem with its stylized griffin, is indeed an excellent example of the Art Deco style of the late twenties.

thanks to its distinctive headlamps. My first reaction was one of despair. The car was dusty and dull and the body full of white streaks from dry polish that had been applied too generously a long time ago. I bent down and crawled under the ropes to take a closer look at the car. It appeared to be original in all details, which changed my mood from despair to hope. I finally realized what a discovery I had made and thought to myself that a thorough cleaning and polishing would make it more photogenic.

Al suddenly rose to his feet. Staring in disbelief at the engine, and with his arms hanging slackly at his sides, he was a picture of total surprise.

"The engine is turned backwards! Did you know? Look, the transmission is in the front. Aha! It's a front-wheel drive. Here is the shift linkage. It goes up there and above the valve covers and through the cowl. And look, there is no gear shift lever on the floor, only a handle on the dashboard. Isn't that something!"

Al had recently joined the museum. His primary responsibility was to keep the music-machines running. So far, he had spent most of his time figuring out their idiosyncrasies. In many of them, old coin-operated pieces, the quarters always got stuck. He had mastered the necessary repair techniques to keep up those machines, but he hadn't had much time to browse among the cars.

Today Al had been assigned to help me put the Ruxton in shape for the picture taking. To him this meant that he was supposed to make it run, which left me in charge of making the Ruxton look good. Now Al had suddenly discovered what a unique car he was dealing with. I dropped the polishing rag again and grabbed the folder, walked around the car to where Al was standing and showed him a cut-away drawing of the transmission.

"Al, take a look at this. See, first and reverse gears are in front of the worm-pinion; second and third are behind. Ruxton was the first front-wheel drive passenger car in America. Although the Cord L-29 was marketed first, Ruxton had announced first. William Muller was the engineer who designed the car. In 1926 he went to his boss at the Budd Body Company in Philadelphia, where he was working as a development engineer, and asked that 15,000 dollars be allocated to develop a front-wheel drive automobile.

By the time the prototype was completed in the fall of 1928, they had spent 35,000 dollars. But it was an extraordinary car, suspended lower than anything else on the road, and everybody was excited about it. Now all they had to do was to sell a manufacturer on the idea of mass producing it. And that's when Archie Andrews came on the scene."

"If I pour some lacquer thinner in the carburetor, I wonder how the engine will react? It's even more explosive than gasoline. It should work, don't you think?"

Al had put together the starter motor again. He had cleaned the spark plugs and reset the gaps. He had gone over all the ignition parts and had changed the condenser. Then he had tried to start the engine, but it didn't want to fire. Now he was contemplating more drastic measures. I wondered if he wanted to know more about the history of the car.

"This Archie Andrews was enormously rich, you see, Al. He had started on Wall Street as a nineteen-year-old and at forty he retired with a fortune of fifty million dollars. He owned an estate in Connecticut and also had a home in California. And he owned the world's fourth largest yacht. It had previously belonged to Henry Ford. This Andrews was a savvy promoter, and he got a group of wealthy people together, among them William Ruxton. Andrews thought Ruxton was a good name for a car, so that's how it came to be called Ruxton."

"Stand back! I'm going to try to start it on the thinner! I don't know what will happen. We may have some fireworks here!"

Al only had to touch the starter button and away she went with a cloud of black smoke bursting out the exhaust pipe. Nobody could remember having seen the car run since 1953. Al grinned triumphantly. Now he had established that there was nothing wrong with the engine. All he needed to work on was getting the gasoline to the carburetor. He turned off the ignition and proceeded to pour thinner in the tank. This would dissolve the old gas in the tank and fuel line, he explained.

"That's very good, Al. Let me tell you more about its history. Andrews got assembly lines going at the Moon Plant and other factories, but these places all went out of business. He finally came to an agree-

ment with Marmon, but then came Black Friday on Wall Street, and everything turned topsy-turvy. Andrews came through it on top, however, and he continued to search for a factory where he could build the Ruxton. But every time he made some progress, the company would fold and finally there was nowhere left to go. Isn't that too bad, Al? Only 300 or 500 Ruxtons were ever made."

Al nodded and poured gasoline in the tank. Fortunately, he had thrown away the cigarette. It had become too short anyway. I stood there with the papers in my hand and watched Al squeeze in behind the wheel. He pressed the starter button, and the Ruxton fired willingly.

"Very interesting history this car has," Al shouted and grinned as he let go of the clutch, spinning the front wheels and sending grass and dirt high in the air as he sped away for a test drive around the building.

I had to agree with Al. This method of demonstrating front-wheel drive was beating all the cut-away drawings in the world!

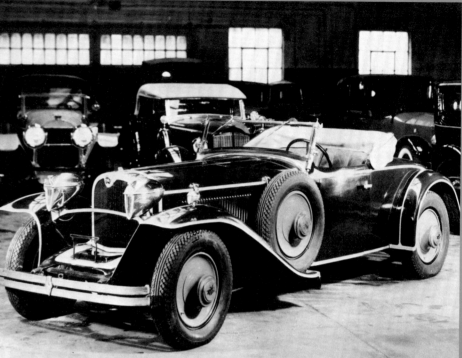

To the upper left appears a rare photograph of a Ruxton assembly line at the Moon plant in St. Louis, Missouri. Notice the unusual striping on the sedan in the foreground. This rainbow color scheme was created by fashionable New York interior designer Joseph Urban and attracted a lot of attention. The picture above shows our "Survivor", later traced to Florida, during the time it was still owned by D. Cameron Peck. The setting is Mr. Peck's garage in Evanston, Illinois, where he housed some 150 cars of the 400 to 600 in his collection. The photograph to the left shows another view of the garage, a sight that today fills every car enthusiast with envy. In the picture to the far left is Mr. Peck and his wife on a 1902 Panhard. This picture was taken on their farm in Baysville, Canada. It was located by the lake, and here Mr. Peck kept some of his other collectibles— classic speed boats. Thanks to Mr. Peck's ambition as a collector, eight Ruxtons were preserved for future generations.

STUTZ

THE LAST GREAT TRAIN CHASER

The maroon Stutz stopped in front of Number Ten North Clark Street. It was eight minutes past five in the afternoon. The streets and sidewalks of Chicago were alive with vehicles and pedestrians on their way home from work. The top of the convertible coupe was folded down, making the automobile look even longer and lower than it actually was. The afternoon sun was hot, and William, unprotected in the open car, removed his hat and wiped his forehead dry. He was just replacing his hat when an elegantly dressed gentleman emerged from the wide double doors of Number Ten. It was early fall, and his light suit was well chosen for the season. He carried a heavy case in his left hand and what looked like rolls of architectural plans under his arm. A raincoat was thrown over the free arm. He wore a white carnation in his lapel.

William moved over to the passenger side when the gentleman came around on the left side and

indicated that he would drive. He sat down behind the wheel, greeted his chauffeur and pulled out a Colt Bluesteel Automatic from the coat pocket. He placed it on the seat between them and draped the coat over the gun. William was not shocked. This was a daily routine. After all, in 1937 Chicago was still America's number one city for crime. And the man with the white carnation was Arthur N. Powers, honorary deputy of the Kankakee Sheriff's Department. He was the law. Mister Powers proceeded to start the Stutz, and then turned to William.

"We should be able to catch her still. What do you think, William?"

"I don't think so, Sir. She has too much of a lead."

Mister Powers smiled as he accelerated, shifting to second gear and then to third. William was not amused. He dreaded these chases more than anything else. The traffic was thinning out as they approached the outskirts of the city, and soon they were on open road driving south towards Kankakee. The highway cut through the fields on an unerring straight line. They were all going parallel—the powerlines, the railroad tracks and the highway. On both sides were corn fields.

Judging from the wind's increasing speed, William thought to himself, we must be doing close to eighty. A glance at the speedometer confirmed his suspicion. Squinting, he carefully scanned the horizon. There was no sign of her.

Arthur N. Powers was a man with a will of his own. He was the oldest of eight children and spent his childhood and youth in Evanston, north of Chicago. He went through grade school and high school without causing his parents undue concern. But when it came time for Arthur to attend Northwestern University, things did not turn out the way they had expected.

His father was a well-known attorney with a successful practice in Chicago, and he naturally wanted to see his oldest son follow in his footsteps. But the courses at Northwestern did not suit Arthur at all. He felt he was wasting his time there. Instead, he enrolled in Metropolitan Business College in Chicago. After completing the required courses, he graduated as a certified accountant.

Once finished with those studies, Arthur acceded to his father's wishes and began to study law. His change in attitude stemmed from the newly formed conviction that he would be able to profitably use legal expertise in his future dealings. He passed the bar examination but decided not to apply for a license to practice.

Arthur finally set out on his own. He soon won influence in financial circles both in Chicago and Boston, and specialized in the brokerage of high-grade municipal, railroad and public utility bonds.

It did not take him long to organize his own utility company, the Illinois Light and Power Company, using proceeds from his successful bond sales. Later he became a financier and, among other large projects, he arranged for the financing of Chicago Stadium. Developer, financier, public utility magnate—that was Arthur N. Powers, the business man.

Arthur's flair for doing things his own way also affected his handling of family matters. In 1913, when he visited Kankakee, his wife revealed many years later, he arrived in an open roadster. It was in the middle of winter, and the snow lay three feet deep. He and his chauffeur drove up in front of the garage where an Italian beauty, Stella Buffo, was employed as the bookkeeper. The two men were dressed in huge fur coats and had buffalo robes thrown over their legs to keep them warm. Arthur took one look at Stella and, in a forthright manner uncommon in those days, asked her if she would care to go out with him for dinner that evening. A couple of years later they were married.

At first, they lived in Chicago and Evanston, but as Arthur prospered he felt it was time for the family, which now included a little daughter, to move away from the growing city. He chose Kankakee. There he found a house which had just been completed, and he decided to purchase it. He reached this conclusion without consulting Stella. In fact, she didn't know anything about his plans to move. But he didn't stop at that. He assigned the fashionable Chicago department store Marshall, Fields and Company to handle the complete decoration of the house. Complete, in Arthur's opinion, included everything from drapes and furniture to dishes and bed linens. When it was

(Continued overleaf)

The charming old photographs on these pages constitute a nostalgic gallery of a bygone era. These were the good old days, when daring and imaginative gentlemen like original Stutz owner Arthur N. Powers were still able to create life styles worthy of their flamboyant tastes. To the left is the man himself, complete with carnation. Above is his beloved Stutz DV-32 parked in front of the family's big white home in Kankakee. To the upper left, the car is parked outside the garage. Standing beside it is the owner dressed for a round of golf. Summer adds a feeling of warmth and happiness to the picture on the right, which shows daughter Gwendolyn with boyfriend and future husband Bruce.

Nostalgic memories were awakened as the 1932 Stutz came roaring down the runway at Santa Paula airport north of Los Angeles. Behind the car, only twenty feet above the ground, Perry Schreffler piloted his Bücker 131 Jungmann biplane to a brief but historic rendezvous between airplane and automobile, captured by the photographer in the picture to the right. The event proved even more significant when it afterwards was discovered that Perry learned to fly in Kankakee, the same small Illinois town where the Stutz' first owner, Arthur N. Powers, used the car for his everyday transportation until the early fifties. In the large picture to the far right, Mr. Powers' grandson, Bruce McBroom, who inherited the Stutz and owns it today, discusses the advantages of ''Dual Valves'' with Perry and admirer in the background, while Bruce's wife, Thea, poses decoratively in the foreground.

all finished, he took Stella to the house and informed her that this was now their home. The house was so completely outfitted that small silver trays filled with candy were placed here and there and fresh flowers decorated every room. Stella was delighted.

In 1932, when his daughter, Gwendolyn, graduated from high school, Arthur's passion for automobiles inspired him to present her with a Stutz Convertible Coupe. It was a grandiose gift, but the car was just too eye-catching for a young girl to drive. So a couple of years later he decided to buy it back from her. He used it for many years. In fact, when his grandson was born he still had it. And when the boy became older, Mister Powers often gave him fifty cents to wax the car, or he took him to the golf course where he would caddy for him. The boy was, of course, fascinated by a man who wore a white carnation in his lapel every day of his life, even when traveling, who smoked Marsh Wheeling cigars, and who could tell stories like nobody else. But the one thing that brought them together in a special way was the Stutz. At this time, in his early childhood, the young grandson didn't know that many years later he himself would be the proud owner of the Stutz. Dedicated family man, gentleman dresser, accomplished golfer, passionate car enthusiast—that was Arthur N. Powers, the private man.

Mister Powers and William had been driving for half an hour before they noticed that they were catching up with her. A dark cloud had appeared on the horizon, and soon they passed patches of smoke drifting along the highway and the railroad tracks. The clouds came to rest in the corn fields, where they slowly dissolved. The sun created long, distinct shadows, and the ones made by the Stutz on the grassy roadside changed form rapidly as the automobile sped by. In the distance they finally saw the train.

"William, there she is! The Green Diamond!"

"Sir, we might as well slow down. We have to stop for gas soon, so we'll never catch her."

"You may be right, William. The needle on the gauge is pointing close to empty, but you never know exactly how much is left in the tank. I think we'll make it!"

The Green Diamond left Chicago at five every afternoon and made its first stop in Kankakee at five fifty-three. Mister Powers used to race the train whenever he had the opportunity. William didn't like it. Now Mister Powers pressed the accelerator slightly, and soon the Stutz was doing ninety. They were driving on a two-way road, and overtaking and passing quite a few cars.

The cars pose no problem, Mister Powers thought to himself as the pulse of the chase intensified. But the farmers with their horse-drawn wagons are a nuisance, he reflected. They enter and turn off and cross the road without regard to the cars, and you have to slow down before passing or the horses will bolt. It doesn't make any difference if you have a sheriff's badge displayed on the car or not. If you scare the horses they will report you no matter who you are, he added.

The highway lay deserted now as far as the eye could see. The Stutz slowly closed the gap behind the Green Diamond, and the smoke became dense and whirled around in increasingly wild patterns. The smell of it made William sick.

They had the train on their right, between them and the sun. When they drove up alongside, they suddenly entered the train's long shadow. The wind became noticeably cooler. Coach by coach they gained on the locomotive. Passengers on the train turned their heads, and some waved. Children ran from window to window to follow the automobile's advance. The train was painted green, and the locomotive was of the latest streamlined design. As the Stutz came up behind it, the engineer turned his head too. He had been resting on his elbow in the open window. Now his face disappeared for a moment. It came back again at the same time the train whistle blew three short signals. A fountain of steam, like a whale spouting off, accompanied the sounds. Mister Powers returned the greeting with three signals from his newly tuned horns. For a moment the locomotive and the car drove side by side and the two men who mastered the magnificent speedmachines exchanged quick glances.

Mister Powers would always savor the moment when he passed the locomotive and entered the warm sunlight again.

The unique photograph to the left shows a racing Stutz ready for action at Pike's Peak outside Denver, Colorado. The driver is believed to be Charles Watts, a Stutz salesman and an uncle of present Stutz owner Bruce McBroom. Notice the gigantic supercharger in front, and the hood ornament proudly carried on top of the radiator. The picture above shows the 1929 Stutz Limousine for many years used by Mr. Powers on his daily commute to Chicago. Standing beside the car, gloves in hand, is the chauffeur William Mine. Pictured to the right is another of Mr. Powers' cars, a 1932 Stutz Convertible Sedan.

THE MAKING OF A MASTERPIECE

"Where were you born?" I asked, pen and paper poised and ready for the answer. Rudy Stoessel and I were sitting in his office at Coachcraft in Hollywood. There were two desks in the small room, both covered with magazines and papers and pieces of body trim from cars in the process of being restored. Mister Stoessel sat in the chair like a man who didn't want to sit. He gave me the impression that he wanted to get back to the Rolls-Royce he had been working on when I arrived.

"In Germany?" I plied him again.

"Nuremberg," he said and reached with his left hand for a box of Tiparillos. I counted seven boxes stacked on top of each other on the desk. Maybe he has just laid in his annual supply, I reflected.

"When were you born and did you grow up in town or in the countryside?" I continued.

"I was born in 1907 in a small town outside Nuremberg. You couldn't even pronounce the name if I told you. What does this have to do with the Darrin Packards, anyway?" he wondered with a sharp look at me. I was beginning to feel a little insecure. He lighted his cigar.

"Oh, I was just curious," I said and tried my luck with still another question. "What's the name of the place?"

"Do you want me to spell it for you?" he asked with irritation as he leaned forward to search the desk for a piece of paper that he felt could be wasted on such an unworthy purpose. He pulled a carpenter's pen from behind his right ear and wrote with large letters. I thought I had caught a glimpse of humor in his eyes. He gave me the paper.

"Herzongenaurach," I read, pronouncing the name of the town in my most casual German.

"You speak German?" he asked, and gave me a skeptical glance.

"Yes, I do. I learned it in school in Sweden, and then I lived in Frankfurt for about half a year when I was twenty," I informed him. I continued to take notes. He nodded and combined a faint smile with a puff on the cigar.

"Tell me about Germany in those days, and what you did, and why you went to America," I asked him, hoping to find an angle of questioning that would make him talk. Not that I wanted to give him the third degree, but I was curious about his background. He was one of those old-world craftsmen, and he had been a very important figure in creating the Packard Darrin.

"I started my apprenticeship as a cabinet maker when I was sixteen. After I finished, I went looking for a job, but there was nothing. Germany had been suffering from terrible inflation, and millions of people went without work. Our family had it pretty good though. We lived in the countryside and grew our own produce, and my parents had a little grocery store. But there was no work for me. One day I asked my old man if I could go to Russia. I had heard that they needed mechanics and carpenters and all kinds of craftsmen. He wouldn't let me go there but said I could go to America if I wanted."

"This was when you were nineteen, so it must have been in 1926. Is that right?" I inquired.

"That's right. I boarded the steamship Columbus at Bremerhafen in 1926. I remember paying a little over two hundred dollars for my third class ticket, and it wasn't very comfortable. The showers only had salt water. They took it directly from the Atlantic. I landed in New York and went through customs and immigration at Ellis Island. From there I went to Buffalo where my aunt lived, and they found a job for me as a cabinet maker. I made eighty-five cents an hour and was for a while quite satisfied."

"It's interesting that while Howard Darrin had gone to Europe a couple years earlier to establish himself

(Continued overleaf)

The photograph above was taken in 1938 and shows Rudy Stoessel in the process of fitting the special aluminum cowl on a partly disassembled Packard body. The work was performed in Howard Darrin's shop on Sunset Boulevard in Hollywood. The cowl, which was the most essential part of the customizing, was patterned for casting by Mr. Stoessel. To the right is the finished product, the Packard Darrin, with Mr. Darrin himself behind the wheel. To the left, a recent photograph of Mr. Stoessel shows him continuing his art in his own shop, Coachcraft of Hollywood.

pictured above, owner Maurice C. Wilson, enjoys the scenery from behind the wheel in his 1941 Packard Darrin, perched on the hillside high above Golden Gate overlooking a sunlit San Francisco. The elegant classic had always been a particular favorite; when he first saw it, he knew this was the car he wanted. His chance came in 1962, and he immediately flew to Los Angeles with two checks in his pocket. One was made out in the amount he had decided to offer, the other was blank—just in case more was needed! The Packard Darrin was an unusual success-story. It was conceived by Howard Darrin, the legendary aviator and automotive designer who based the prototypes on a Standard Packard chassis. After some fifteen cars had been built by his own shop in Hollywood, the car became so sought-after that Packard was obliged to come up with a production model to meet the demand.

in the coach building business, you came to America to learn the trade," I interjected.

"Yes, it seems backwards. My first job in the coach building business came when I went to Pierce-Arrow. I had heard that they paid a buck an hour, so I thought I would try. I got hired at once to work in their experimental shop building prototypes and other special cars. I worked for Pierce until Studebaker took them over, and we in the experimental shop were told to work on the assembly line or not work at all. I chose to quit. But before this happened, I remember finishing a special limousine for President Hoover's inauguration."

"So this was your first contact with automobiles." I commented. He was talking quite enthusiastically now, and it was obvious that he was beginning to enjoy the dive into his memory. I was beginning to appreciate his special kind of humor, and my self-confidence was restored.

Mister Stoessel stroked his graying hair from his forehead back to his neck, and continued telling me about his early experiences in America.

"Yes, that was my first real contact with cars. My parents never owned one, but I remember looking at an Opel in Germany before I went to the States. If I had only had the money! But enough of that. When I quit at Pierce, 'wanderlust' overcame me, and I decided to go to California. Three of my friends and I took the Greyhound bus across the continent. We stopped in Cleveland and Chicago and Denver. I tell you, we had a good time! We sang on the bus and played guitar and mandolin."

"Who played the mandolin?" I wondered.

"None of your business," he said jokingly but aggressively and tried to hide his embarrassment. "When we arrived at the bus depot in Los Angeles I had only twenty-five bucks in my pocket, and I blew that money in Mexico the first weekend we were there, when we went to Tijuana. Somehow I made it back to Los Angeles and started to walk around to the different furniture shops to see if they had any openings for a cabinet maker. Bluebird Furniture on Alameda Street hired me. I made sixty cents an hour. It wasn't much, but at least I had enough for food. This was 1929 you have to remember, and there were already a lot of people without work."

"When did you get back to coach building again?" I asked in an effort to swing the conversation back to the experiences leading up to his work on the Darrin.

"That came next. I went to Kirchhoff in Pasadena. He had been general manager for Murphy Coach-builders before he started his own shop. When he heard that I had worked for Pierce he gave me a job immediately, and I made a buck an hour again. One of the cars I remember working on there was a front-wheel drive Miller for a man in Santa Barbara. We had only ninety days to finish the job and Kirchhoff wanted me to make the pattern for casting the windshield frame. I had never done this before, but he gave me some books on the subject and it turned out all right."

"You also built L-29 Cords, didn't you?" I sidetracked.

"Yes, but that was when I worked for Fuller. He was the Auburn-Cord-Duesenberg dealer and had a shop on West Market Street in Los Angeles. We built two cars for E. L. Cord himself. One was a coupe, the other one a towncar."

"So by now you were really established as a well-known craftsman in the coach building business?" I inserted.

"Yes and no. The worst was yet to come. I went back to Kirchhoff again for a while, where we built a Duesenberg touring towncar for a woman by the name of Ingraham. This was in 1932 when the depression really hit hard. When we finished the Duesenberg I had to look for another job. At Kirchhoff I had made a buck twenty-five, but now I had to be satisfied with forty cents. Soon I was out of work for good. I managed to get twelve hundred dollars on my life insurance and lived on that for a year until I got a job again building armored cars, ambulances, Coca-Cola trucks and so on."

"Just for orientation, what year was this?" I wondered.

"It must have been 1938, because it was when I was working on a refrigerated milk truck at Standard Auto Body that Howard Darrin walked in one day and asked if I wanted to work for him. He had two special Packards under way at Crown Coach, but he wasn't happy with their work and wanted to set up his own shop. He had leased a place on Sunset where

Sunbeam Market is today, and I went with him to look it over. I was fully convinced when he showed me his twenty-five thousand dollar bank account.''

''So you completed those two first Packard Darrins?'' I continued.

''Yes, those two were for Clark Gable and Chester Morris. They created so much demand that Darrin decided to make a series of them. The concept was to use as many stock body panels as possible from the standard eight-cylinder Packard but then rework them to give an effect of a complete custom design. The most important element in the process was the special cowl. It was a kind of centerpiece. Darrin made the drawings, and I interpreted them. A new windshield was done the same way. The alterations also included custom doors, new seat structures, top bows and modifications to the rear deck.''

''How exactly did you make the cowl?'' I asked.

''It was made in three sections: the top and the two sides. I made the patterns out of wood exactly the way I wanted the finished aluminum casting to look. But the tricky part was that the pattern had to allow for shrinkage. Aluminum shrinks three sixteenths per foot when it cools off. So the patterns had to be made that much larger. The finished pattern was then turned over to the foundry. They put it in some kind of mixture of molasses and sand and then filled the impression with melted aluminum. That was the first casting. It had to be cleaned and finished off perfectly and then another casting was made. That was the final one.''

''And in 1939 it was time to start your own business?'' I continued. That year Howard Darrin had been asked by the Packard Company to move to Connersville, Indiana, where he was to direct the factory production model of Packard Darrins. He closed down his shop, and Mister Stoessel was out of work again. But this time he was well established. And he started Coachcraft with two of his co-workers. Today, more than thirty years later, he is still going strong.

''It was a good thing you didn't go to Russia.'' I said jokingly as the interview came to an end.

And he said, ''Oh, I would have become a commissar, I'm sure!'' throwing his head back in a good laugh.

Featured in these photographs are different models of the early Packard Darrin. The picture above shows one of them parked on a movie lot in Hollywood. Mr. Darrin found most of his customers among the movie-making set—stars like Clark Gable and Chester Morris. This particular car came out at the end of the series, at which time the runningboards were eliminated. To the left, two Darrins are parked outside the shop on Sunset Boulevard. Notice the presence of the runningboards. To the right is a frontal view. It is interesting to compare this photo with the frontal view on the previous color spread. This reveals the differences between the original Darrins made in Hollywood and the factory production run from Connersville.

PIERCE-ARROW

ONE FOR THE ROAD AND ONE FOR THE SHOW

The gray clouds had been hanging low over Pebble Beach since early morning. Usually the California spring was sunny and dry. But once in a while you would have a day of overcast, and then you could never know if it would rain or not. On this particular Saturday in 1955, however, it was especially important that the rain stay away. And so far it had. Not a single splashmark blemished the shiny surfaces of the cars displayed on the lawn in front of Del Monte Lodge where the annual Concours d'Elegance was approaching its grand finale. Judges were adding up scores while spectators gathered in growing numbers around the cars, waiting for the winners to be announced. A band provided background music and if, for a moment, you became tired from looking at all the automotive elegance, you could sit down by the edge of the terrace and watch the waves of the Pacific as they exploded against the cliffs below.

One hundred of the most outstanding cars on the West Coast had been accepted by the show. Many applicants had been turned away since only the absolute best were shown here. In those days it was unusual to see restored cars. Of course, there were the new paint jobs and the re-upholstered interiors, but the standards for restorations as we know them today had not yet been set. This year, however, judges and spectators would encounter a trendsetter. Most of the cars in the show were in well-kept original condition. This was the case with a 1934 Rolls-Royce Phantom II from Los Altos. Although it had 120,000 miles on the odometer, it was judged to be nearly perfect. There were also quite a few new cars. One could admire, for instance, a gleaming
(Continued overleaf)

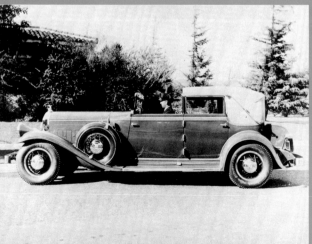

The photograph to the left was taken in 1931 as the Pierce-Arrow was delivered to Phil Hill's aunt. Her home in Santa Monica can be seen in the background. In the color pictures on the following pages, the house and the car are shown as they appear today, almost fifty years later. In the picture above, four-year-old Phil is captured beside the Pierce with his brother Jerry. To the right, Phil accepts the award for best of show at Pebble Beach in 1955. He was called away from his practice for next day's road race and didn't have time to change his clothes, which explains his casual appearance.

Racing ace Phil Hill, one of the most successful American drivers on national, as well as international circuits, is the owner of this 1931 Pierce-Arrow. The magnificent "Survivor" has been in the family's possession since new. The photographs on this spread were taken in Santa Monica, California, with the Pierce parked exactly where it was delivered to Mr. Hill's aunt. The house in the background, for many years occupied by the aunt, was the scene of memorable experiences with the Pierce; as a teenager young Phil occasionally managed to "steal" the big automobile away for a few fast laps around the block. Later he used the Pierce for his everyday transportation to and from school, and it was, of course, excellent for dating purposes. He drove the car until it became time to try "racier wheels". In 1955 Mr. Hill was among the trend-setters when he decided to give the Pierce a radical facelift, making it one of the first classics to receive a "ground-up" restoration. Pierce-Arrow was considered one of the most aristocratic cars of its day. Proof of this fact is certainly given by the restrained yet elegant styling of this one-of-a-kind Town Cabriolet by Le Baron.

1955 Alfa Romeo. There was even a convertible Volkswagen. But the top honors in the event were usually captured by the Rolls-Royces.

Pebble Beach offered the automotive enthusiast an entire weekend of pleasures. While the Concours was the attraction on Saturday, the Roadrace was the scene of action on Sunday. An exciting but dangerous course was used for this race. It curved in and out among the trees along the beautifully wooded coastline and was, of course, even more treacherous when wet. Practice was going on during the Concours, and the crowd viewing the cars could hear the screaming engines in the distance as the Ferraris and Jaguars and Austin-Healeys circled the course in preparation for the following day's event.

All the favorites had gathered for the occasion. Last year's winner, Sterling Edwards, was there. So was Bill Pollack, who won the race in 1951 and 1952. Phil Hill, winner of the 1950 and 1953 races, just back from his near-victory at Sebring, was also there.

But Phil was not only a contender in the race. He had also entered his 1931 Pierce-Arrow in the show. This car had been owned by his aunt since new. It was based on a Le Baron convertible, but his aunt had ordered it specially built for her as a towncar, complete with glass partition.

Phil could remember the Pierce when it was delivered at his aunt's house in Santa Monica. He lived just a few blocks away, and at the age of four he was an often-seen visitor there. His aunt used it for more elegant occasions, but also for long trips across the continent to Florida. The car stayed there with her for months at a time. One such journey had etched itself into Phil's memory in a special way. They were driving across the Everglades with his uncle behind the wheel. Phil and his aunt occupied the passenger compartment. As they passed through the most desolate areas with swamps on both sides of the road, they were caught in a terrible rainstorm. Phil and his aunt were well protected, but his uncle fared badly in the chauffeur's compartment. Both he and the engine were totally soaked with water. As a result, it began to misfire. It was impossible to continue driving until the water had dried.

Phil's aunt used it less frequently at the end of the thirties, and finally it spent more time on blocks than it did on the road. This period in the car's history coincided with Phil's arrival at legal driving age. He took over the car in 1943 and used it for his everyday commutes to and from school. In 1947 he bought his first MG, and the Pierce was retired.

During these years of hard use the Pierce had deteriorated and this process continued even after it had been stored away. Phil was sad to see it in this state. He and his brother often talked about fixing it up. But it was not until 1954 that this thought became a reality. The original intention was for the Pierce to receive a simple face lift, but as the dismantling continued and they dove deeper and deeper into it, the project soon changed its objective, the goal now becoming restoration to its perfect original condition.

Work progressed rapidly in the Hill garage. While the chassis was sanded and brushed, other parts were being chromed. Finally all the details were ready for assembly. When this phase was complete, the time-consuming work of refurbishing the interior began. The carpets alone proved to be a challenge. Three different sets were supplied to fit different conditions; a leather-bound snapover pile-carpet for normal uses, a leather-bound rubber carpet for wet weather and another one for the most exclusive occasions. This was a soft carpet of unborn lamb's wool. Part of the luxurious comfort was also a lap robe of hair from the shaved belly of a baby beaver.

The woodwork and the leather were also refinished. New wiring was installed, but the original system was kept, down to the intercom between driver and passenger. Then finally, nine months after the body had first been lifted off the chassis, the Pierce was ready.

Phil's Pierce-Arrow proved to be just the car to upset the Rolls-Royce dominance at the Concours. Spectators and judges agreed. They called the Pierce, "probably the most beautifully restored car ever seen in the United States". A new standard was set.

When the judges had come to a decision, a message was sent to Phil. He was in the process of tuning his Ferrari Monza in the pits. The message requested him to come immediately to Del Monte Lodge. The Pierce had won the top honor, and the award was waiting for him, as well as was the crowd, the message went on. Phil took a quick look at himself. His pants were dirty and wrinkled. And he wore an

old sweater and sport shirt. But there was no time to change.

The photographs taken from the award presentation show the gleaming Pierce surrounded by a crowd of connoisseurs. Beside the car stands a beautiful lady, dressed in the latest fashion from Rome or Paris. She is just handing over the winner's plaque. Only one thing is out of place—Phil, in his wrinkled pants and worn sweater. But nobody cared about a minor detail like that. Phil was pleased with his unexpected success. So was the crowd.

But Saturday's event was only the beginning of an action-filled weekend for Phil. Sunday started out with the same gray clouds hanging over Pebble Beach as had been there Saturday. But instead of keeping back the rain, they now began to pour it out over the circuit and the 20,000 spectators.

When the starting flag dropped, it was raining so heavily that the competitors had to turn on the headlights so the cars could be seen by the drivers behind. Pollack shot away like a rocket in his Baldwin Special. Phil was second, and third was Edwards in his Ferrari Monza. Phil was moving up close to Pollack and stayed there. The spray from the churning rear wheels soaked Phil's face and shoulders. For ten laps the battle went on until finally Phil's Ferrari came around as the leader. Pollack tried to hang on but his car wasn't able to and he drove into the pits on lap 22. From there on it was Phil Hill's race. When he was flagged off as the winner, he had lapped all his competitors, and was 30 seconds away from doing it again. As the winner began to strip off his drenched clothing, the mechanic reached down in the cockpit. His hand sank to the wrist in water.

The Pebble Beach weekend was dominated by Phil's successes. But he was to go on to even bigger things. In 1958 one of his dreams, of winning Le Mans, became a reality. And then an even more impossible dream, the world championship, was realized in 1961. During these years he did not forget his love for classic cars. When he retired from racing he went into full-time restoration, setting up shop in Santa Monica. His own classics go on winning Concours awards. So do all the cars he restores for connoisseur car-owners all over the nation.

To Phil Hill the Le Mans victory in 1958 was a success beyond his wildest expectations. In the picture to the left he is captured by the camera with an expression that shows both exhaustion and contentment. He had just crossed the finishing line as the winner after driving continuously for the last six hours. The rain pours down as Phil guides his Ferrari through one of the turns at Le Mans in the picture above. At times he had to sit on the toolbox in order to improve visibility. The photograph to the right shows Phil in the cockpit of the Ferrari Monza he drove at Palm Springs in 1955.

CHRYSLER

RECOLLECTIONS AT THE ROADSIDE

It was very cold and I could see my own breath while I talked to the three men waiting beside the Chrysler.

"Do you think he will come? He wasn't in his office at the museum this morning. I called downtown but he wasn't there either. They told me he had the flu."

"Maybe he stayed home," said one of the men.

"If he promised to be here, he will be here. You can count on that. I know him," another one assured me.

The three men were all dressed in the same kind of white shop coat with "Harrah's Automobile Collection" embroidered on the back. They held their hands in their pockets and moved their feet all the time to keep up their circulation while they waited. I was already freezing. I had come up from Los Angeles for the day and hadn't thought of the difference in temperature. The ski-jacket I had borrowed from one of the men helped quite a bit, but I was still cold. I decided I had to do something about it.

"I'm freezing to death. I'd better move around," I said and left the men. I made several short rushes down the road, breathing through my mouth and looking like a locomotive.

While I worked my body hard to keep from freezing, I concentrated my mind on the man I would soon meet, William Harrah, the creator of one of the world's largest gaming operations and also, more important to me, the founder of the world's largest automobile collection. Mister Harrah had shown unusually mature business sense already dur-

The photograph above, showing William Harrah and his parents beside a 1922 Franklin, was taken during a family vacation in Yosemite National Park, California. Pictured to the left is William's first car, a Chevrolet. He had equipped it with thirteen lights and seven horns, all according to latest teenage fashion. The sequence to the right illustrates the hazards of winter driving. The pictures were taken in the early thirties at Big Bear Lake in the San Bernardino Mountains, California. Mr. Harrah, tall and confident, stands beside the Franklin in the first picture. In the next he prepares to crawl out the window.

ing his college years when he bought out his father's interest in a Bingo parlor in Southern California. A few years later he started another one in Reno. He had six employees at this time. In 1946 he was ready to open his first casino. It was located right on famous Virginia Street in Reno. From there the operation grew with meteoric speed. I had heard figures quoted illustrating the scope of Harrah's of today. He now employs more than 6,000 during peak season. Almost as many are guests on an average night at the "Big Name Shows" introduced by Harrah. On some occasions, 30,000 people have been served during one day in all the restaurants and coffee shops.

The Automobile Collection began in 1948 with the acquisition of a 1911 Maxwell and a Ford of the same vintage. He added cars as often as he found one worth buying. In 1962 the Collection opened its doors to the public. Today it contains more than 1,500 cars and receives 350,000 visitors annually. Harrah employs almost 100 craftsmen in his restoration shop. He is still looking for cars, and he still personally supervises the restoration of every car and test-drives the finished product before he gives the final stamp of approval.

I had been told that Mister Harrah rarely agreed to interviews and even more seldom consented to have his picture taken.

A few weeks ago when I had been in touch with one of Mister Harrah's assistants, I had explained to him what I was doing and that I wished to feature the Chrysler and Mister Harrah in my book. The assistant promised to take it up with Mister Harrah, but he didn't think there was much of a chance that he would agree to do it. And based on what I had been told, I didn't think so myself. But he did agree. And the Chrysler had been in the detailing shop since nine this morning, pedantically attended to by the three men in white coats, and now Mister Harrah was supposedly on his way here.

For the setting I had chosen a deserted stretch of road on one of the softly sloping hills outside Reno. There should have been snow on the ground this time of year, but it had been an unusual season in Nevada, and all over the western states, for that matter. Instead of the white snow there were still the ripe
(Continued overleaf)

William Harrah picked this 1931 Chrysler Imperial in 1961 to be purchased for his collection. He felt that the powerful and elegant automobile had long been under-rated and was indeed worthy of inclusion with other of the classic automobiles in his collection. A snowless Nevada winter landscape surrounds the world's leading car collector and his Chrysler in the double page photograph on previous color spread. In the pictures on these pages the Chrysler displays its sleek and graceful profile. The divided windshield was a new styling feature that year. The leather upholstery, carried all the way up and over the top of doors and cowl, as can be seen in the picture to the left, added to the luxurious feeling of the cock pit. This stylish automobile was indeed a bargain for just over $3,000 as it cost new, especially considering that a Packard or a Lincoln was priced over $5,000 and a Duesenberg often cost five times as much as a Chrysler.

colors of fall. I looked at the black Chrysler and beyond it. First there was the golden, dry grass. It began at the roadside where the car was parked. Then there was the blue of the water in the creek running parallel to the road, and then more grass with trees here and there. The trunks were dark brown or sometimes black, and the branches were bare. Then there was more grass for a long distance as I let my eyes follow the flow of the hillside. And far away was the blue of the mountains. Even they were snowless.

I was right in the middle of one of my quick rushes, running back towards the Chrysler, when I heard the sound of an approaching car. I turned my head and saw the red Ferrari just as it rounded the curve further down the road behind me. The low car accelerated and sped by with a high-pitched racing sound. It passed the Chrysler and parked on the other side of it. I reached the Chrysler at the same time the driver of the Ferrari unfolded his tall frame.

"He's here!" one of the men told me, and they all looked attentive now and ready for action. I walked toward the Ferrari and met Mister Harrah halfway.

"I hear you aren't feeling well today?"

"I'm fine," he said and looked at the Chrysler, "where do you want me?"

I described to him the different angles I had in mind and we started. I felt good when I looked in the viewfinder. I could see that the pictures would turn out fine. I continued for quite a while, taking frame after frame. The men in the white coats were moving the step-ladder for me, and in between the different takes they hurried up to the car to polish some chrome detail, or to remove a leaf, or a fingerprint, or something else they had discovered. Mister Harrah and I were talking back and forth about where he should hold his hands or where he should look. We had been going on like that for quite a while when one of the men in white approached me and whispered in my ear.

"You better let him go now. It's not good for him to be outside in the cold." I nodded and took a few more frames, then went up to Mister Harrah where he sat behind the wheel in the Chrysler.

"Are you cold?"

"No, I'm fine."

"Well, I'm finished anyway. It's freezing out here and you have a cold and I've kept you here too long already."

"How come you chose the Chrysler for your book?"

"I just like the way it looks."

"I do too. It's a very elegant automobile. Look at the leather upholstery here. Look at the way it's drawn up over the doors and the cowl. Isn't that beautiful. We bought it fifteen years ago from a man in Utah. It was in good shape, and we kept it displayed until a few years ago when it had a total restoration."

"Wasn't your first car a Chrysler?"

"No, I wanted one badly but my father wouldn't let me. He felt that I shouldn't have a car that was better than what the other kids had. I can't remember what Brad drove, but Harry had a Chevy and Felix a Star. My father gave me a Chevy. It was a 1926 Roadster and I was only fifteen. I shortened the rear springs and put on straight pipes. I remember that it was Brewster Green and had yellow disk wheels and yellow stripping. We were nuts on accessories. I had thirteen lights and seven horns on it! We lived in Hollywood then. My special trick was to turn on the road using the handbrake. Mulholland was dirt then, you see. I must have been arrested once a week for speeding."

Mister Harrah talked in a soft-spoken way. His voice did not reveal his feelings, but the words did.

They communicated the nostalgic value these memories had to him. I asked what became of the Chevy.

"One time I was late to a football game. I left the key in the car and when I came back after the game was over, the car was gone. Stolen. It was recovered a couple of weeks later. The lights and the horns were removed, and who knows what else they had done to it. The car wasn't the same to me anymore, so I sold it."

"Speaking of speeding. The Ferrari must be a temptation to a man who likes to drive fast," I said and became aware of the man in white winking at me, probably again trying to make me understand that Mister Harrah shouldn't be kept out in the cold any longer.

"Nowadays it's different. You have to be very careful. But you should have been around in the thirties. I had just started here in Reno then and for a while I had my family in southern California, so there was a lot of driving between here and Los Angeles. I remember one time I was caught speeding. I must have been doing eighty or ninety. This was on the way up around Bishop. I was driving a 1936 Zephyr with a two-speed rear end. They called it the Columbia rear end. Anyway, I was to appear in court. I had heard of the judge before. He was really tough on speeders. Anyway, I went there. I think it was in a little place called Lone Pine. There was this little old country judge and I happened to mention the Columbia rear end. And he said, 'them darn things really get away from you, don't they. I know, I have one myself.' And then he said, 'the least I can give you is a ten dollar's fine.'"

We all laughed and Mister Harrah stepped out of the Chrysler. I thanked him for taking time, and for coming out in spite of his cold. The Ferrari turned around and passed the Chrysler on the way back. There was a quick glance from Mister Harrah and a no-nonsense gesture from his hand.

"Boy, this is the first time I've heard him tell stories about himself," said one of the men in white.

The red Ferrari disappeared behind the tall grass as it went around the curve further down the road. I saw the red roof a few more times as the car rapidly gained speed and disappeared in the distance.

Eugene Dutro, standing in front of the car in the picture above, drove this Chrysler Imperial Eight from Columbus to Hebron, Ohio, averaging 98 mph. The distance was 22 miles, and it was believed at the time to be the fastest average ever attained by a stock car on a highway in America. Another stock car record holder, Billy Arnold, poses beside the Chrysler he drove at Daytona Beach in the spring of 1931. He was also the winner of the 1930 Indianapolis 500 race. The small picture to the right shows Mr. Harrah's Chrysler as it appeared when it arrived at Reno in 1961.

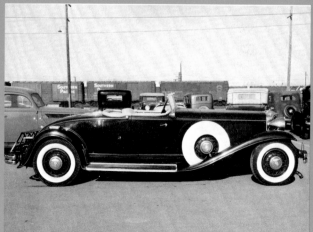

FRANKLIN

LETTERS FROM THE MERRIMAC FILE

The darkness of the desert night had totally invaded the house except for Tom's study, where the desk lamp was spreading a soft pyramid of light. He was alone, that is, if you excluded Beaver, Tom's Golden Retriever. The dog was asleep on the floor under the desk. His rhythmic breathing was the only sound in the room.

Tom opened the yellow file laying in front of him. A sudden desire to look at some of the Merrimac letters had overcome him as he was preparing to go to bed this evening. Now he was sitting at his desk.

Tom had built quite a collection of Franklin memorabilia over the years. It contained original factory drawings of chassis and engines, rare photographs of Franklins in elegant showrooms from the Twenties and Thirties when the dealers decorated them with exotic palms and oriental rugs. They looked more like sets from *Casablanca* than showrooms as we think of them today, Tom reflected, as he tried to visualize the different items in his growing collection. There were also stacks of original sales literature, clippings and articles, and several drawers of cor-

respondence files with letters to and from Franklin enthusiasts.

Tom had always been a Franklin enthusiast. He could clearly remember when he was five years old, and his father owned a 1929 Franklin Convertible Coupe. They had bought it in 1930 when they were still living in Tulsa, Oklahoma. His father was a geologist, and traveled extensively in his business. Sometimes young Tom would go with him. These were the earliest of his Franklin memories.

The next thing he could remember was a trip to Syracuse, New York. He had accompanied his mother to the factory there to pick up a new Franklin. This was in 1933 and Tom was eight years old. His father had ordered the car with special leather upholstery and radio. The antenna was hidden under the running board, Tom remembered. But what happened on the way back to Oklahoma made the greatest impression on him.

It was a long journey, and they drove all day and into the night to save time. When they were on a desolate stretch of road in Missouri, his mother became aware of a pair of headlights in the rearview mirror. There was very little traffic this time of the night, so she could easily determine if another car was following them. Tom was sleeping in the back seat, and when his mother later told him what had happened, he wished he had been awake. The car behind them had come up very close as if it wanted to pass, then had fallen back again as if the driver had noticed something. Then the car had tried to drive up alongside again, but an approaching truck had forced it back again. By now Tom's mother had become really worried and she pressed the gas pedal to the floor, but the lights behind them were still just as close. Finally they had reached a gas station. Tom could remember waking up to the sound of loose gravel hitting the wheel wells when they left the road. He sat up just in time to catch a glimpse of the mystery car as it slowly passed with the headlights turned off. He thought he had seen two men with slouchy hats in the car. When his mother told the gas station attendant about the incident, he said that there had been many hold-ups in the area lately. One of the truck drivers at the station offered to come with

them to Rolla, the nearest town. He had a revolver, and this made Tom's mother feel safe.

Tom grew up and his interest in cars was still there, but it took quite a few years before he became actively involved. He remembered one occasion which could have been a triggering experience. In 1951 he visited the James Melton Museum—the first prominent automobile museum. There he had admired a 1911 Franklin Limousine.

A year later he happened to come across a photograph showing a Dual Cowl Franklin. Tom thought it was the most beautiful Franklin he had ever seen. The car became an image of the ultimate. Then, by coincidence, he saw a picture of the car again, this time in a book mentioning that the Franklin was owned by a certain Helge Anderson of Bridgeport, Connecticut. Tom could not erase the car from his mind, and in 1953 he wrote to the owner. Tom made it clear that he was extremely anxious to buy it and would like to have the first chance, should Anderson ever decide to sell. Maybe Tom never really thought the car would ever become his, because he bought a V-12 Brougham instead. Just afterwards he received an offer from Anderson. The man wanted 800 dollars for it, but Tom had spent all his money on the Brougham and had to let it go. The Franklin instead went to Robert Thompson of Westport, Connecticut.

In 1956 Tom went to see Thompson. The owner of the Franklin stated he would never sell the car but maybe he would consider a trade if he was tempted with a certain Bentley. Tom thought of this as a definite no. First of all, those Bentleys were almost impossible to get. You had to find one in England, if you could find one at all. Secondly, Tom thought, the man would probably change his mind once he was confronted with the Bentley. Tom returned, disappointed, to his home in Tucson, where he had now moved.

From time to time the Franklin came back to mind, and again by coincidence, he saw a photograph of it. This was in a 1931 magazine. It stated that the car was a one-of-a-kind built by Merrimac Body Company in Merrimac, Massachusetts. It had been commissioned by a Stillman Kelley of Lexington, (Continued overleaf)

Pictured at the top of the left hand page is an American Bantam and the Franklin Merrimac in 1942 at original owner Stillman Kelley's home in Massachusetts. Below is the Franklin in 1956 when it belonged to Robert Thompson. Below this picture is a snapshot of frame and body during the 1974 restoration. The photograph above was taken by the coach-builder after the masterpiece was completed. To the right Mr. and Mrs. Kelley occupy the front seat again after 27 years, photographed by present owner Tom Hubbard at the Kelley's Virginia home. Ron Lorenson, who worked with Hubbard on the restoration, rests in the back seat.

Proper for an environment as torrid as the Arizona desert is an aircooled automobile like this 1931 Franklin. The pioneer carmaker at this time already had thirty years of experience in manufacturing aircooled engines. The small picture to the left shows how Franklin engineers solved the problem of pre-heating the mixture in an aircooled engine: the exhaust and inlet ports are on opposite sides of the heads, but the exhaust pipe turns in front of the engine and runs back past a hot-spot above the carburetor. The "Survivor" featured here has a one-of-a-kind dual cowl body by Merrimack and is regarded as the most beautiful of all Franklins. Long-time Franklin enthusiast Thomas H. Hubbard had his eyes on this car for many years but was unable to persuade the owner to part with it until he located a Bentley in England which met the specifications of the owner and finally tempted him to trade. In the picture above, Tom's golden retriever, Beaver—a member, like his master, of the Franklin Club—takes his seat in anticipation of a rough drive along dusty Tucson roads.

Massachusetts. From now on Tom thought of the car as "The Merrimac".

Tom leaned forward and searched in the file for a postcard he remembered receiving in 1960. It was from Robert Thompson, and it read:

"I still have the car, and it is as happy as could be . . . although some friends tell me that I tightened a bit too much on a tappet and have a skip. Maybe, but if so, I shall fix it.

I could not even consider selling it, but I just might be able to be talked into it if someone would wave a Three Liter Old School Bentley with Van den Plas Tourer body in my face. I am sick and tired of unreliable old cars and if I should ever loose the Franklin, I would want another reliable one . . . but a fast one, too.

If you can get a good Bentley, I might think."

After this message Tom began to believe that there was something to this idea of Thompson's. He wrote back and wanted a more definite confirmation. There was another letter in the file from Thompson:

"Now, as I said in the card . . . I am being hard to get along with. I mean just that, for what I would like is for you to locate that Bentley, for you to buy it, for you to ship it into the country, and then we could make the swap.

Again, my Franklin is not for sale, but for swap. You do the work. I have a genuine goody there. I am hard to get—the car is hard to get. If you still wish to go ahead on these 'tough guy' terms, fine."

There was a post script added to the letter, and Tom now read it with a smile:

"I am not that nasty, really. I just like the car even more than you, if that's possible."

Tom got busy. He ran ads in several magazines in England, finally located a Bentley of the exact specifications, arranged for its shipment to New York where Thompson met him, and the transaction was completed.

Later, when Tom drove it home to Arizona, everything went fine except for thirteen flat tires. Tom thought of it now, and reflected that it was the valve stems that caused the trouble. Tom was extremely satisfied with the car, the fact that it was finally his, and that he owned the world's most beautiful

Franklin. Now he began looking into its past. He located Stillman Kelley, the original owner, and wrote to him. The file contained a letter from Kelley in response to Tom's letter. It read:

"The car was ordered in the early spring of 1931. I was planning to be married in June and had hopes of having the car for our wedding trip. However, that was not to be and I got delivery of it, as well as I can remember, around the end of July or the first of August. Our trip was taken in a 1929 Franklin Convertible instead. However, to get back to the Phaeton, it was more or less copied from the Cadillac Twelve model of that time. I tried out the Cadillac but did not like its roadability as you had to fight it around curves whereas the Franklin took them with ease. As you know, Franklin made very little in the way of open cars so I merely took the bull by the horns and got that open job.

A few highlights that might interest you are that several times I had the car up to 93 by its speedometer with the top up but never had it over 88 with the top down. However, even when I sold the car after sixteen years, it would cruise from 65-75 without any trouble and that over winding Maine roads. Needless to say, it rode like a baby carriage and it was, I thought, a most perfectly balanced car on the road."

Tom corresponded with Kelley for many years, and in 1974 they finally met in Camden, Maine, at Kelley's summer place where the Merrimac had spent much of its life. Then in 1975, Tom once again drove the car across the country, stopping en route at the Kelley's Virginia home. It was a sentimental reunion for Kelley and his old car after 27 years, and Tom was happy that he could photograph the now restored car with the man who had caused it to be created in the first place.

It was getting very late now. Tom closed the file and put it back in the drawer. The Golden Retriever came around the desk and looked at his master. Tom patted the dog on the head and let him know that he agreed it was long past their bedtime, and that they were now finally going to quit this silly reading business. Tom leaned forward and turned off the light. The base of his desk lamp was made from a section of the wooden frame of an old Franklin.

To the left, Tom Hubbard, present owner of the Franklin Merrimac, is pictured during a trip with his father in a 1929 Franklin Convertible Coupe. The rock behind the rear wheel was a common sight in those early days. Another common sight were roads like the one above, the transcontinental highway outside Amarillo, Texas, with the same Franklin. In the picture to the right, two Franklins are in hot pursuit through Death Valley. This was a publicity stunt of the early twenties arranged by the Franklin people to disprove accusations from the competition that the aircooled Franklins would overheat in hot weather.

ANATOMY OF A CAR LOVER

The fall of 1929 saw many significant events. Some were of consequence only to isolated individuals. Other happenings would affect an entire nation of people.

Bob Allen was only four years old that fall. And to him it was a significant event when his father took a picture of him standing beside the family's black and maroon Essex. Bob was not sure if he should smile or be serious. But he knew what to do with his hands; they belonged in his pockets. His sister Victoria was also in the picture, and he noted with disapproval how strangely she acted, showing uninhibited excitement about having her picture taken. To Bob the fact that he was photographed with the car was the important thing. The cold autumn wind caught Bob's tie just as Mister Allen pressed the shutter release. At that moment Bob had still not made up his mind whether to smile or not.

To Bob's father, however, who was a travelling salesman for an investment firm, the collapse of the stock market was the significant event that fall. The Allen family lived in Charlotte, North Carolina, and they had been able to make a good living from what the father brought home. The last couple of years had turned Wall Street into the focus of attention, and fortunes could be made there. It was no longer a playground for just the financial aristocracy. Now the man on the street could invest in American business

and try his luck among professional speculators. The prices of stock skyrocketed as people flocked around this modern golden calf. The stock of Radio Corporation of America, for instance, went from one hundred dollars per share to five hundred within a few months.

Mister Allen loved cars. He was extremely pleased with the Essex. But he had used it for three years now, and it was time to replace it. The Essex people were very successful in marketing their products. In 1929 Essex and its companion, Hudson, managed to capture a position among the five biggest sellers. Mister Allen had ordered a new car already before the events on Wall Street. This time he had chosen a Hudson Brougham with custom body by Biddle and Smart. It had sidemounted spare tires and landau irons on the rear quarter. Mister Allen transmitted his love for cars to his son, and when the Hudson arrived, Bob thought it was the most exciting thing that had ever happened in his young life. He could hardly wait for the day to come when he would be able to drive it himself.

But the stockmarket crash put an end to the good life. A crash of another kind put an end to the Hudson. Over the years it had developed a bad habit. At the speed of fifty the front wheels would suddenly begin to vibrate violently. It was impossible to control the steering and the speed had to be reduced immediately. There were no provisions for adjusting or balancing the wheels, so Mister Allen just had to live with the problem. But an accident was bound to happen sooner or later. When it did, the car almost ran off a bridge. Fortunately, they made it across, and the Hudson instead went into the embankment on the other side. As a result of the accident, however, the family's Hudson era came to an end in the spring of 1933. That year also marked the end of the Hoover administration and the beginning of Roosevelt's "New Deal". The "New Deal" for Mister Allen was a Dodge four-door sedan. Bob was eight now and growing more and more eager to try the wheel himself.

Americans experienced turbulent years as the nation pulled itself out of the economic depression. A new optimism became evident. Bad things ended and good things started. In 1933 prohibition was finally abolished. The next year marked the beginning

of the end of the gangster-era when John Dillinger was shot to death by federal agents in Chicago. The Social Security Bill was sent to the Senate in 1935. That same year Packard introduced the new "Junior Series" at the Auto Show in New York. These smaller cars were designated "One Twenty" after the length of the wheelbase and became an instant success.

In 1936, Mister Allen was able to afford one of these new Packards, a touring sedan. The Dodge was now to be used by Bob's mother. Two years later the Packard was traded in for a new one. This was also a sedan, dark blue with an optional trunk rack. Bob's father was an avid quail-hunter and converted the trunk to a dog pen. His two pointers, Dan and Kate, made many trips in that accommodation.

Bob was now thirteen. He often asked his father about driving, but was always told that he could not expect to try the wheel before he had reached the legal age of sixteen. It was a difficult wait. And he was constantly on the lookout for an opportunity to shorten it.

During the summers he often stayed with his grandparents in Batesburg, South Carolina. One time an aunt came for a visit in her Plymouth. Bob saw an opportunity. He managed to talk the aunt into letting him drive. And then he located a deserted place and after two weeks of repeated sessions on that dirt road, Bob had learned the secrets of driving an automobile long before he was officially supposed to. He was very pleased.

Bob Allen was four years old when his father took the picture to the upper left. Bob's sister Victoria joins the young car enthusiast in front of the family's 1926 Essex. The photograph above shows Bob in Germany during the last part of the war. As an administrator of a medical unit, he had the privilege of driving this 1941 Pontiac. Back again in the United States, he used his army earnings to buy himself his first car, a 1947 Nash 600. The picture to the left features the proud owner. To the right is Bob's next car, a 1942 Lincoln. It was black, he paid 950 dollars for it, and got twenty miles to the gallon.

Just as the American people began to feel used to the blue sky of their newfound optimism, the dark clouds began to gather again. In 1938 Hitler marched into Austria, and in the fall of 1939 came the invasion of Poland. In the spring of 1940 Denmark, Norway, Holland, Belgium and France were occupied. America was still not involved and most people preferred to believe that they would be able to stay that way. In 1940 Mister Allen bought a new flat-head V-8 Ford. It was black. Then, in 1941, came Pearl Harbor.

1944 brought a big change in Bob's life. He was now nineteen and Uncle Sam wanted him. The Army sent him to Germany to help with the liberation. He was stationed in Saint Magnus, a small town outside Bremen. Together with some friends he found a 1939

(Continued overleaf)

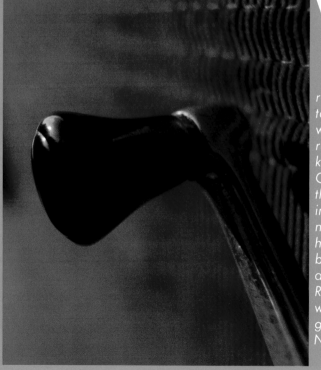

When Edsel Ford returned from a trip to Europe in 1938, he came back with ideas for an automobile he wanted built for himself. A few cars were made based on Zephyr chassis and body components. These cars were received with so much enthusiasm that it was decided to put the model into production. From the dashboard with its gold macoid trim around instruments and radio speaker grill to the ruby-colored plastic door-knobs and the upholstery in maroon whipcord, the Continental projected a new concept formulated like this in the original sales catalog: "Everything implied in the name is expressed in the design of this the newest and most striking of the Lincoln Zephyrs. For here is a car, different from anything in America, built for those who want to go places that are far away . . . and go in swift luxurious comfort." Owner Robert F. Allen and his daughter were photographed with the 1940 Lincoln Zephyr Continental on the grounds of Chancelot Stables outside Charlotte, North Carolina.

Opel hidden in a barn. The "liberation" of this car meant nothing more than a thorough cleaning which revealed a light blue paint job and a well preserved vehicle. It was used without license plates. Nobody said anything about it. Gasoline was also "liberated", allowing the car to be used for all "necessary" transportation. As the administrator of a regimental medical unit, Bob was also entitled to the use of a 1941 Pontiac. It was painted in the obligatory olive-green color, and it was the first car he drove equipped with column shift.

Bob returned from Germany in 1946. He had saved most of what he had earned in the army, and now he had a sizable sum of money ready to stimulate the postwar economy. But Bob did not buy stock or land. He bought a car. He chose a Nash 600 Sedan. Bob practically lived in this car, and it took him only sixteen months to wear it out. He had a habit of always driving as fast as he possibly could and the six-cylinder engine just couldn't take the punishment.

By now Bob attended Vanderbilt University in Nashville, Tennessee. When the Nash gave up, he replaced it with a 1942 Lincoln Sedan. It was the smoothest car he had ever driven. And it was quiet. Even when he went outside to listen for the engine he could hardly hear it running.

Although he was very pleased with his car, he had at this time already seen the ultimate Lincoln. At the start of the first semester one of the students had arrived in a chauffeur-driven dark blue Continental. Bob was stunned by the beauty of this car.

Some time later an encounter with another Continental would reinforce his impression. He was in Nashville and just happened to spot a big white convertible on the other side of the street. He crossed over to take a closer look. While in the process of carefully studying the car from all angles, the owner surprised him in the act. The car belonged to singer Roy Acuff. He seemed flattered by Bob's interest in the car and ended up giving him the keys so he could take a test-ride on his own. Startled by this generosity, Bob asked what would happen if he decided not to come back. Mister Acuff told him laughingly that he would not be hard to spot with the only white Continental in the South. The drive lasted fifteen minutes. The memory lasted much longer.

Bob bought another Lincoln in 1950. It was a one-year-old Cosmopolitan Sedan. The car was painted a gun metal gray and was of the rare slip stream model. It had overdrive and radio with foot operated channel selector. Bob owned this car until 1954 when he acquired a brand new Mercury Coupe.

For many years Bob would now experience a period of his life when the cars he owned did not mean as much to him. Maybe it was the fact that he was married and had children. Or maybe all the energy he had to expend to establish his business took away his interest for cars. However, it seemed to him that the cars had changed. There was no love put into them anymore when they were made and, therefore, you could not feel love for them anymore when you owned them, he decided. For whatever reason, the new cars could not bring him the same satisfaction as the cars of his youth had done.

One day many years later when Bob's business was well established and his children had grown up, he received a call from a close friend who was aware of his feelings for old cars. The friend thought Bob would be interested to know that there was a 1940 Continental for sale in High Point. This town was only a couple of hours drive to the north of Charlotte. Bob decided to take a look at it that same evening. When the light was turned on in the garage and he saw the Continental, he knew he wouldn't return home without it.

The Continental was a Convertible and was painted in silver and had a maroon interior. Instead of the standard upholstery of all leather or a combination of leather and whipcord, this one had an all whipcord interior. The owner showed him the original shipping invoice which indicated that this was the way it had been ordered. The Lincoln had been put back in original shape a few years ago, one of the first Continentals to receive a thorough restoration.

There was never any doubt in Bob's mind as to whether he wanted the car or not. The entire transaction took only fifteen minutes. Bob looked at the old invoice. It was dated June 20, 1940.

That was just about the time when I learned to drive, he thought to himself.

The unique Continental in the picture to the left is the number two prototype, manufactured in June of 1939, and now in the process of being restored by its owner, Jessie Haines of Ambler, Pennsylvania. The car was used for road testing by the Engineering Department. Afterwards it was owned by Bob Gregory, who together with Edsel Ford, was responsible for the styling of the Continental. The number one prototype was so full of mechanical defects it was later scrapped, making Mr. Haines' car the earliest surviving Continental. The pictures above and right show two Cabriolets as Ford's Advertising Department and Vogue Rubber Company projected them to the public.

"The Survivors" was photographed, written and designed by Henry Rasmussen. Assistant designer was Walt Woesner. Typesetting was supplied by Holmes Typography of San Jose. The color-separations were produced by Graphic Arts Systems of Burbank. Zellerbach Paper Company supplied the 100-pound Flokote stock, manufactured by S. D. Warren. Litho Craft of Anaheim printed the book, under the supervision of Brad Thurman. The binding was provided by National Bindery of Pomona.